Answers to Prayer

From GEORGE MÜLLER'S NARRATIVES

COMPILED BY A. E. C. BROOKS

First published in 1897 by THE MOODY PRESS

This edition published December 2025

Illustrations copyright Pastor Joe Lighthall, 2025

"I never remember, in all my Christian course, a period now (in March, 1895) of sixty-nine years and four months, that I ever SINCERELY and PATIENTLY sought to know the will of God by *the teaching of the Holy Ghost*, through the instrumentality of the *Word of God*, but I have been ALWAYS directed rightly. But if *honesty of heart* and *uprightness before God* were lacking, or if I did not *patiently* wait upon God for instruction, or if I preferred *the counsel of my fellow men* to the declarations of *the Word of the living God*, I made great mistakes."

GEORGE MÜLLER.

PREFACE

Mr. Brooks, in this compilation, has endeavoured to select those incidents and practical remarks from Mr. Müller's Narratives, that show in an unmistakeable way, both to believers and unbelievers, the secret of believing prayer, the manifest hand of a living God, and His unfailing response, in His own time and way, to every petition which is according to His will.

The careful perusal of these extracts will thus further the great object which Mr. Müller had in view, without the necessity of reading through the various details of his "Narratives," details which Mr. Müller felt bound to give when writing periodically the account of God's dealings with him.

For those who have the opportunity, an examination of the *"Autobiography of George Müller, or, a Million and a Half in Answer to Prayer"* will richly repay the time spent upon it.

Mr. Müller gave permission for the compilation of this volume.

HOW TO ASCERTAIN THE WILL OF GOD

1. I seek at the beginning to get my heart into such a state that it has no will of its own in regard to a given matter. Nine-tenths of the trouble with people generally is just here. Nine-tenths of the difficulties are overcome when our hearts are ready to do the Lord's will, whatever it may be. When one is truly in this state, it is usually but a little way to the knowledge of what His will is.

2.—Having done this, I do not leave the result to feeling or simple impression. If so, I make myself liable to great delusions.

3.—I seek the Will of the Spirit of God through, or in connection with, the Word of God. The Spirit and the Word must be combined. If I look to the Spirit alone without the Word, I lay myself open to great delusions also. If the Holy Ghost guides us at all, He will do it according to the Scriptures and never contrary to them.

4.—Next I take into account providential circumstances. These often plainly indicate God's Will in connection with His Word and Spirit.

5.—I ask God in prayer to reveal His Will to me aright.

6.—Thus, through prayer to God, the study of the Word, and reflection, I come to a deliberate judgment according to the best of my ability and knowledge, and if my mind is thus at peace, and continues so after two or three more petitions, I proceed accordingly. In trivial matters, and in transactions involving most important issues, I have found this method always effective.

GEORGE MÜLLER

CHAPTER I

BEGINNING AND EARLY DAYS OF THE ORPHAN WORK

"That the trial of your faith, being much more precious than of gold that perisheth, though it be tried with fire, might be found unto praise and honour and glory at the appearing of Jesus Christ."—1 Peter, i. 7.

MR. GEORGE MÜLLER, the founder of the New Orphan-Houses, Ashley Down, Bristol (institutions that have been for many years the greatest monuments of modern times to a prayer-answering God), gives in that most valuable and instructive book, *"A Narrative of Some of the Lord's Dealings with George Müller,"* Vol. I., among other reasons for establishing an Orphan-House, the following:—

"Sometimes I found children of God tried in mind by the prospect of old age, when they might be unable to work any longer, and therefore were harassed by the fear of having to go into the poorhouse. If in such a case I pointed out to them, how their Heavenly Father has always helped those who put their trust in Him, they might not, perhaps, always say, that times have changed; but yet it was evident enough, that God was not looked upon by them as the LIVING God. My spirit was ofttimes bowed down by this, and I longed to set something before the children of God, whereby they might see, that He does not forsake, even in our day, those who rely upon Him.

"Another class of persons were brethren in business, who suffered in their souls, and brought guilt on their consciences, by carrying on their business, almost in the same way as unconverted persons do. The competition in trade, the bad times, the over-peopled country, were given as reasons why, if the business were carried on simply according to the word of God, it could not be expected to do well. Such a brother, perhaps, would express the wish, that he might be differently situated; but very rarely did I see *that there was a stand made for God, that there was the holy determination to trust in the living God, and to depend on Him, in order that a good conscience might be maintained.* To this class likewise I desired to show, by a visible proof, that God is unchangeably the same.

"Then there was another class of persons, individuals who were in professions in which they could not continue with a good conscience, or persons who were in an unscriptural position with reference to spiritual things; but both classes feared, on account of the consequences, to give up the profession in which they could not abide with God, or to leave their position, lest they should be thrown out of employment. My spirit longed to be instrumental in strengthening their faith, by giving them not only instances from the word of God, of His willingness and ability to help all those who rely upon Him, but *to show them by proofs*, that He is the same in our day.

"I well knew *that the Word of God ought to be enough*, and it was, by grace, enough, to me; but still, I considered that I ought to lend a helping hand to my brethren, if by any means, by this visible proof to the unchangeable faithfulness of the Lord, I might strengthen their hands in God; for I remembered what a great blessing my own soul had received through the Lord's dealings with His servant A. H. Franke, who in dependence upon the living God alone, established an immense Orphan-House, which I had seen many times with my own eyes.

" I, therefore, judged myself bound to be the servant of the Church of God, in the particular point on which I had obtained mercy: namely, *in being able to take God by His word and to rely upon it.*

"All these exercises of my soul, which resulted from the fact that so many believers, with whom I became acquainted, were harassed and distressed in mind, or brought guilt on their consciences, on account of not trusting in the Lord; were used by God to awaken in my heart the desire of setting before the church at large, and before the world, a proof that He has not in the least changed; and this seemed to me best done, by the establishing of an Orphan-House.

"It needed to be something which could be seen, even by the natural eye. Now, if I, a poor man, simply by prayer and faith, obtained *without asking any individual*, the means for establishing and carrying on an Orphan-House, there would be something which, with the Lord's blessing, might be instrumental in strengthening the faith of the children of God, besides being a testimony to the consciences of the unconverted, of the reality of the things of God.

"This, then, was the primary reason for establishing the Orphan-House. I certainly did from my heart desire to be used by God to benefit the bodies of poor children, bereaved of both parents, and seek in other respects, with the help of God, to do them good for this life;—I also particularly longed to be used by God in getting the dear orphans trained up in the fear of God; —but still, the first and primary object of the work was (and still is:) that God might be magnified by the fact, that the orphans under my care are provided with all they need, only by *prayer and faith* without anyone being asked by me or my fellow-labourers whereby it may be seen, that God is FAITHFUL STILL, and HEARS PRAYER STILL.

"That I was not mistaken, has been abundantly proved since November, 1835, both by the conversion of many sinners who have read the accounts, which have been published in connection with this work, and also by the abundance of fruit that has followed in the hearts of the saints, for which from my inmost soul, I desire to be grateful to God, and the honor and glory of which not only is due to Him alone, but, which I, by His help, am enabled to ascribe to Him."

"OPEN THY MOUTH WIDE."

In the account written by Mr. Müller dated Jan. 16, 1836, respecting the Orphan-House intended to be established in Bristol in connection with the Scriptural Knowledge Institution for Home and Abroad, we read:

"When, of late, the thoughts of establishing an Orphan-House, in dependence upon the Lord, revived in my mind, during the first two weeks I only prayed that if it were of the Lord, he would bring it about, but if not that He graciously would be pleased to take all thoughts about it out of my mind. My uncertainty about knowing the Lord's mind did not arise from questioning whether it would be pleasing in His sight, that there should be an abode and Scriptural education provided for destitute fatherless and motherless children; but whether it were His will that I should be the instrument of setting such an object on foot, as my hands were already more than filled. My comfort, however, was, that, if it were His will, He would provide not merely the means, but also suitable individuals to take care of the children, so that my part of the work would take only such a portion of my time, as, considering the importance of the matter, I might give, notwithstanding my many other engagements. The whole of those two weeks I never asked the Lord for money or for persons to engage in the work.

"On December 5th, however, the subject of my prayer all at once became different. I was reading Psalm lxxxi., and was particularly struck, more than at any time before, with verse 10: "*Open thy mouth wide, and I will fill it.*" I thought a few moments about these words, and then was led to apply them to the case of the Orphan-House. It struck me that I had never asked the Lord for anything concerning it, except to know His will, respecting its being established or not; and I then fell on my knees and opened my mouth wide, asking Him for much. I asked in submission to His will, and without fixing a time when He should answer my petition. I prayed that He would give me a house, *i. e.*, either as a loan, or that someone might be led to pay the rent for one, or that one might be given permanently for this object; further, I asked Him for £1000; and likewise for suitable individuals to take care of the children. Besides this, I have been since led to ask the Lord, to put into the hearts of His people to send me articles of furniture for the house, and some clothes for the children. When I was asking the petition, I was fully aware what I was doing, *i. e.*, that I was asking for something which I had no natural prospect of obtaining from the brethren whom I know, but which was not too much for the Lord to grant."

"December 10, 1835.—This morning I received a letter, in which a brother and sister wrote thus:—"We propose ourselves for the service of the intended Orphan-House, if you think us qualified for it; also to give up all the furniture, &c., which the Lord has given us, for its use; and to do this without receiving any salary whatever; believing that if it be the will of the Lord to employ us, He will supply all our needs, &c."

"Dec. 13.—A brother was influenced this day to give 4s. per week, or £10 8s. yearly, as long as the Lord gives the means; 8s. was given by him as two weeks' subscriptions. To-day a brother and sister offered themselves, with all their furniture, and all the provisions which they have in the house, if they can be usefully employed in the concerns of the Orphan-House."

A GREAT ENCOURAGEMENT.

"Dec. 17.—I was rather cast down last evening and this morning about the matter, questioning whether I ought to be engaged in this way, and was led to ask the Lord to give me some further encouragement. Soon after were sent by a brother two pieces of print, the one seven and the other 23¾ yards, 6¾ yards of calico, four pieces of lining, about four yards altogether, a sheet, and a yard measure. This evening another brother brought a clothes horse, three frocks, four pinafores, six handkerchiefs, three counterpanes, one blanket, two pewter salt cellars, six tin cups, and six metal tea spoons; he also brought 3s. 6d. given to him by three different individuals. At the same time he told me that it had been put into the heart of an individual to send to-morrow £100."

ONE THOUSAND POUNDS.

"June 15, 1837.—To-day I gave myself once more earnestly to prayer respecting the remainder of the £1000. This evening £5 was given, so that now the whole sum is made up. To the Glory of the Lord, whose I am, and whom I serve, I would state again, that every shilling of this money, and all the articles of clothing and furniture, which have been mentioned in the foregoing pages, have been given to me, *without one single individual having been asked by me for anything*."

ORPHANS FOR THE BUILDING.

In a third statement, containing the announcement of the opening of the Orphan-House, for destitute female children, and a proposal for the establishment of an Infant Orphan-House, which was sent to the press on May 18, 1836, Mr. Müller wrote:—

"So far as I remember, I brought even the most minute circumstances concerning the Orphan-House before the Lord in my petitions, being conscious of my own weakness and ignorance. There was, however, one point I never had prayed about, namely that the Lord would send children; for I naturally took it for granted that there would be plenty of applications. The nearer, however, the day came which had been appointed for receiving applications, the more I had a secret consciousness, that the Lord might disappoint my natural expectations, and show me that I could not prosper in one single thing without Him. The appointed time came, and not even one application was made. I had before this been repeatedly tried, whether I might not, after all, against the Lord's mind, have engaged in the work. This circumstance now led me to lie low before my God in prayer the whole of the evening, February 3, and to examine my heart once more as to all the motives concerning it; and being able, as formerly, to say, that His glory was my *chief aim*, *i. e.*, that it might be seen that it is not a vain thing to trust in the living God,—and that my *second aim* was the spiritual welfare of the orphan-children,—and the *third* their bodily welfare; and still continuing in prayer, I was at last brought to this state, that I could say *from my heart*, that I should rejoice in God being glorified in this matter, though it were by *bringing the whole to nothing*. But as still, after all, it seemed to me more tending to the glory of God, to establish and prosper the Orphan-House, I could then ask Him heartily, to send applications. I enjoyed now a peaceful state of heart concerning the subject, and was also more assured than ever that God would establish it. *The very next day*, February 4, the first application was made, and since then 42 more have been made."

"JUST FOR TODAY."

Later on, when there were nearly 100 persons to be maintained, and the funds were reduced to about £20, Mr. Müller writes:—

"July 22 [1838].—This evening I was walking in our little garden, meditating on Heb. xiii. 8, "Jesus Christ the same yesterday, and today, and for ever." Whilst meditating on His unchangeable love, power, wisdom, &c.—and turning all, as I went on, into prayer respecting myself; and whilst applying likewise His unchangeable love, and power and wisdom, &c., both to my present spiritual and temporal circumstances:— all at once the present need of the Orphan-House was brought to my mind. Immediately I was led to say to myself, Jesus in His love and power has hitherto supplied me with what I have needed for the Orphans, and in the same unchangeable love and power He will provide me with what I may need for the future. A flow of joy came into my soul whilst realising thus the unchangeableness of our adorable Lord. About one minute after, a letter was brought me, enclosing a bill for £20. In it was written: "Will you apply the amount of the enclosed bill to the furtherance of the objects of your Scriptural Knowledge Society, or of your Orphan Establishment, or in the work and cause of our Master in any way that He Himself, on your application to Him, may point out to you. It is not a great sum, but it is a sufficient provision for the exigency of to-day; and it is for *to-day's* exigencies, that, ordinarily, the Lord provides. Tomorrow, as it brings its demands, will find its supply, etc."

"[Of this £20 I took £10 for the Orphan fund, and £10 for trip other objects, and was thus enabled to meet the expenses of about £34 which, in connection with the Orphan-Houses, came upon me within four days afterwards, and which I knew beforehand would come.]"

WAITING FOR HELP.

"Nov. 21, 1838.—Never were we so reduced in funds as to-day. There was not a single halfpenny in hand between the matrons of the three houses. Nevertheless there was a good dinner, and by managing so as to help one another with bread, etc., there was a prospect of getting over this day also; but for none of the houses had we the prospect of being able to take in bread. When I left the brethren and sisters at one o'clock, after prayer, I told them that we must wait for help, and see how the Lord would deliver us this time. I was sure of help, but we were indeed straitened. When I came to Kingsdown, I felt that I needed more exercise, being very cold; wherefore I went not the nearest way home, but round by Clarence Place. About twenty yards from my house, I met a brother who walked back with me, and after a little conversation gave me £10 to be handed over to the brethren, the deacons, towards providing the poor saints with coals, blankets and warm clothing; also £5 for the Orphans, and £5 for the other objects of the Scriptural Knowledge Institution. The brother had called twice while I was gone to the Orphan-Houses, and had I now been *one half minute* later, I should have missed him. But the Lord knew our need, and therefore allowed me to meet him. I sent off the £5 immediately to the matrons."

BEYOND DISAPPOINTMENT.

"Sept. 21 [1840], Monday. By what was in hand for the Orphans, and by what had come in yesterday, the need of to-day is more than supplied, as there is enough for to-morrow also. To-day a brother from the neighbourhood of London gave me £10, to be laid out as it might be most needed. As we have been praying many days for the School,—Bible,—and Missionary Funds, I took it all for them. This brother knew nothing about our work, when he came three days since to Bristol. Thus the Lord, to show His continued care over us, raises up new helpers. They that trust in the Lord shall never be confounded! Some who helped for a while may fall asleep in Jesus; others may grow cold in the service of the Lord; others may be as desirous as ever to help, but have no longer the means; others may have both a willing heart to help, and have also the means, but may see it the Lord's will to lay them out in another way;—and thus, from one cause or another, were we to lean upon man, we should surely be confounded; but, in leaning upon the living God alone, we are *BEYOND disappointment, and BEYOND being forsaken because of death*, or *want of means*, or *want of love*, or *because of the claims of other work*. How precious to have learned in any measure to stand with God alone in the world, and yet to be happy, and to know that surely no good thing shall be withheld from us whilst we walk uprightly!"

A GREAT SINNER CONVERTED.

In his REVIEW OF THE YEAR 1841, Mr. Müller writes:—

"During this year I was informed about the conversion of one of the very greatest sinners, that I ever heard of in all my service for the Lord. Repeatedly I fell on my knees with his wife, and asked the Lord for his conversion, when she came to me in the deepest distress of soul, on account of the most barbarous and cruel treatment that she received from him, in his bitter enmity against her for the Lord's sake, and because he could not provoke her to be in a passion, and *she would not* strike him again, and the like. At the time when it was at its worst I pleaded especially on his behalf the promise in Matthew xviii. 19: 'Again I say unto you, that if two of you shall agree on earth as touching anything that they shall ask, it shall be done for them of my father which is in heaven.' And now this awful persecutor is converted."

PRAYER FOR SPIRITUAL BLESSING AMONG THE SAINTS.

"On May 25th, I began to ask the Lord for greater real spiritual prosperity among the saints, among whom I labour in Bristol, than there ever yet had been among them; and now I have to record to the praise of the Lord that truly He has answered this request; for, considering all things, at no period has there been more manifestation of grace and truth, and spiritual power among us, than there is now while I am writing this for the press (1845). Not that we have attained to what we might; we are far, very far from it; but the Lord has been very, very good to us, and we have most abundant cause for thanksgiving."

WITHHOLDING THE REPORT.

"Dec. 9 [1841].—To-day came in for the Orphans by the sale of stockings 10s. 10d.—We are now brought to the close of the sixth year of this part of the work, *having only in hand the money which has been put by for the rent*; but during the whole of this year we have been supplied with all that was needed.

"During the last three years we had closed the accounts on this day, and had, a few days after, some public meetings, at which, for the benefit of the hearers, we stated how the Lord had dealt with us during the year, and the substance of what had been stated at these meetings was afterwards printed for the benefit of the church at large. This time, however, it appeared to us better to delay for a while both the public meetings and the publishing of the Report. Through grace we had learned to lean upon the Lord only, being assured, that, if we were never to speak or write one single word more about this work, yet should we be supplied with means, as long as He should enable us to depend on Himself alone. But whilst we neither had had those public meetings for the purpose of exposing our necessity, nor had had the account of the Lord's dealings with us published for the sake of working thereby upon the feelings of the readers, and thus inducing them to give money, but only that we might by our experience benefit other saints; yet it might have appeared to some that, in making known our circumstances, we were actuated by some such motives. What better proof, therefore, could we give of our depending upon the living God alone, and not upon public meetings or printed Reports, than that, *in the midst of our deep poverty*, instead of being glad for the time to have come when we could make known our circumstances, we still went on quietly for some time longer, without saying anything. We therefore determined, as we sought and still seek in this work to act for the profit of the saints generally, to delay both the public meetings and the Report for a few months. *Naturally* we should have been, of course, as glad as anyone to have exposed our poverty at that time; but *spiritually* we were unable to delight even then in the prospect of the increased benefit that might be derived by the church at large from our acting as we did.

"Dec. 18. Saturday morning. There is now the greatest need, and only 4d. in hand, which I found in the box at my house; yet I fully believe the Lord will supply us this day also with all that is required.— Pause a few moments, dear reader! Observe two things! We acted *for God* in delaying the public meetings and the publishing of the Report; but *God's way leads always into trial, so far as sight and sense are concerned. Nature* always will be tried *in God's ways.* The Lord was saying by this poverty, 'I will now see whether you truly lean upon me, and whether you truly look to me.' Of all the seasons that I had ever passed through since I had been living in this way, *up to that time*, I never knew any period in which my faith was tried so sharply, as during the four months from Dec. 12, 1841, to April 12, 1842. But observe further: We might even now have altered our minds with respect to the public meetings and publishing the Report; *for no one knew our determination, at this time*, concerning the point. Nay, on the contrary, we knew with what delight very many children of God were looking forward to receive further accounts. But the Lord kept us steadfast to the conclusion, at which we had arrived under His guidance."

"HE ABIDETH FAITHFUL."

Under the date Jan. 25, 1842, Mr. Müller writes:—

"Perhaps, dear reader, you have said in your heart before you have read thus far: 'How would it be, suppose the funds for the Orphans were reduced to nothing, and those who are engaged in the work had nothing of their own to give, and a meal time were come, and you had no food for the children.'

"Thus indeed it may be, for our hearts are

desperately wicked. If ever we should be so left to ourselves, as that either we depend no more upon the living God, or that 'we regard iniquity in our hearts,' then such a state of things, we have reason to believe, would occur. But so long as we shall be enabled to trust in the living God, and so long as, though falling short in every way of what we might be, and ought to be, we are at least kept from living in sin, such a state of things cannot occur. Therefore, dear reader, if you yourself walk with God, and if, on that account, His glory is dear to you, I affectionately and earnestly entreat you to beseech Him to uphold us; for how awful would be the disgrace brought upon His holy name if we, who have so publicly made our boast in Him, and have spoken well of Him, should be left to disgrace Him, either by unbelief in the hour of trial, or by a life of sin in other respects."

DELAYED BUT SURE.

"March 9 [1842].—At a time of the greatest need, both with regard to the Day-Schools and the Orphans, so much so that we could not have gone on any longer without help, I received this day £10 from a brother who lives near Dublin. The money was divided between the Day-Schools and the Orphan-Houses. The following little circumstance is to be noticed respecting this donation:—As our need was so great, and my soul was, through grace, truly waiting upon the Lord, I looked out for supplies in the course of this morning.

"The post, however, was out, and no supplies had come. This did not in the least discourage me. I said to myself, the Lord can send means without the post, or even now, though the post is out, by this very delivery of letters He may have sent means, though the money is not yet in my hands. It was not long after I had thus spoken to myself, when, according to my hope in God, we were helped; for the brother who sent us the £10, had this time directed his letter to the Boys' Orphan-House, whence it was sent to me."

"LIKE AS A FATHER."

"March 17.—From the 12th to the 16th had come in £4 5s. 11½d. for the Orphans. This morning our poverty, which now has lasted more or less for several months, had become exceedingly great. I left my house a few minutes after seven to go to the Orphan-Houses, to see whether there was money enough to take in the milk, which is brought about eight o'clock. On my way it was specially my request that the Lord would be pleased to pity us, even as a father pitieth his children, and that He would not lay more upon us than He would enable us to bear, I especially entreated Him that He would now be pleased to refresh our hearts by sending us help. I likewise reminded Him of the consequences that would result, both in reference to believers and unbelievers, if we should have to give up the work because of want of means, and that He therefore would not permit of its coming to nought. I moreover again confessed before the Lord that I deserved not that He should continue to use me in this work any longer. While I was thus in prayer, about two minutes' walk from the Orphan-Houses, I met a brother who was going at this early hour to his business. After having exchanged a few words with him, I went on; but he presently ran after me, and gave me £1 for the Orphans. Thus the Lord speedily answered my prayer. Truly, it is worth being poor and greatly tried in faith, for the sake of having day by day such precious proofs of the loving interest which our kind Father takes in everything that concerns us. And how should our Father do otherwise? He that has given us the greatest possible proof of His love which He could have done, in giving us His own Son, surely He will with Him also freely give us all things."

TRUST IN THE LORD BETTER THAN MAN'S PROMISES.

"May 6 [1845].—About six weeks ago intimation was kindly given by a brother that he expected a certain considerable sum of money, and that, if he obtained it, a certain portion of it should be given to the Lord, so that £100 of it should be used for the work in my hands, and the other part for Brother Craik's and my own personal expenses. However, day after day passed away, and the money did not come. I did not trust in this money, yet, as during all this time, with scarcely any exception, we were more or less needy, I thought again and again about this brother's promise; though I did not, by the grace of God, trust in the brother who had made it, but in the Lord.

"Thus week after week passed away, and the money did not come. Now this morning it came to my mind, that such promises ought to be valued, in a certain sense, as nothing, *i. e.*, that the mind ought never for a moment to be directed to them, but to the living God, and to the living God only. I saw that such promises ought not to be of the value of one farthing, so far as it regards thinking about them for help. I therefore asked the Lord, when, as usual, I was praying with my beloved wife about the work in my hands that He would be pleased to take this whole matter, about that promise, completely out of my mind, and to help me, not to value it in the least, yea, to treat it as if not worth one farthing, but to keep my eye directed only to Himself. I was enabled to do so. We had not yet finished praying when I received the following letter:

——May 5, 1845

Beloved Brother,

Are your bankers still Messrs. Stuckey and Co. of Bristol, and are their bankers still Messrs. Robarts and Co. of London? Please to instruct me on this; and if the case should be so, please to regard this as a letter of advice that £70 are paid to Messrs. Robarts and Co., for Messrs. Stuckey and Co., for you. This sum apply as the Lord may give you wisdom. I shall not send to Robarts and Co. until I hear from you.

Ever affectionately yours——

"Thus the Lord rewarded at once this determination to endeavour not to look in the least to that promise from a brother, but only to Himself. But this was not all. About two o'clock this afternoon I received from the brother, who had more than forty days ago, made that promise, £166 18s., as he this day received the money, on the strength of which he had made that promise. Of this sum £100 are to be used for the work in my hands, and the remainder for brother Craik's and my own personal expenses."

Under date 1842 Mr. Müller writes:—

"I desire that all the children of God, who may read these details, may thereby be lead to increased and more simple confidence in God for everything which they may need under any circumstances, and that these many answers to prayer may encourage them to pray, particularly as it regards the conversion of their friends and relatives, their own progress in grace and knowledge, the state of the saints whom they may know personally, the state of the church of God at large, and the success of the preaching of the Gospel. Especially I affectionately warn them against being led away by the device of Satan, to think that these things are peculiar to me, and cannot be enjoyed by all the children of God; for though, as has been stated before, every believer is not called upon to establish Orphan-Houses, Charity Schools, etc., and trust in the Lord for means; yet all believers are called upon, in the simple confidence of faith, to cast all their burdens upon Him, to trust in Him for everything, and not only to make every thing a subject of prayer, but to expect answers to their petitions which they have asked according to His will, and in the name of the Lord Jesus.—Think not, dear reader, that I have *the gift of faith*, that is, that gift of which we read in 1 Cor. xii. 9, and which is mentioned along with 'the gifts of healing,' 'the working of miracles,' 'prophecy,' and that on that account I am able to trust in the Lord. *It is true* that the faith, which I am enabled to exercise, is altogether God's own gift; it is true that He alone supports it, and that He alone can increase it; it is true that, moment by moment, I depend upon Him for it, and that, if I were only one moment left to myself, my faith would utterly fail; but *it is not true* that my faith is that gift of faith which is spoken of in 1 Cor. xii. 9 for the following reasons:—

"1. The faith which I am enabled to exercise with reference to the Orphan-Houses and my own temporal necessities, is not that 'faith' of which it is said in 1 Cor. xiii. 2 (evidently in allusion to the faith spoken of in 1 Cor. xii. 9), 'Though I have all faith, so that I could remove mountains, and have not charity (love), I am nothing'; but it is the self-same faith which is found in *every believer*, and the growth of which I am most sensible of to myself; for, by little and little, it has been increasing for the last sixty-nine years.

"2. This faith which is exercised respecting the Orphan-Houses and my own temporal necessities, shows itself in the same measure, for instance concerning the following points: I have never been permitted to doubt during the last sixty-nine years that my sins are forgiven, that I am a child of God, that I am beloved of God, and that I shall be finally saved; because I am enabled, by the grace of God, to exercise faith upon the word of God, and believe what God says in those passages which settle these matters (1 John v. 1—Gal. iii. 26—Acts x. 43—Romans x. 9, 10—John iii. 16, etc.)....

"Further, when sometimes all has been dark, exceedingly dark, with reference to my service among the saints, judging from natural appearances; yea, when I should have been overwhelmed indeed in grief and despair, had I looked at things after the outward appearance; at such times I have sought to encourage myself in God, by laying hold in faith on His mighty power, His unchangeable love, and His infinite wisdom, and I have said to myself: God is able and willing to deliver me, if it be good for me; for it is written: "He that spared not His own Son, but delivered Him up for us all, how shall He not with Him also freely give us all things?" Rom. viii. 32. This, this it was which, being believed by me through grace, kept my soul in peace.

"Further, when in connection with the Orphan-Houses, Day Schools, etc., trials have come upon me which were far heavier than the want of means when lying reports were spread that the Orphans had not enough to eat, or that they were cruelly treated in other respects, and the like; or when other trials, still greater, but which I cannot mention, have befallen me in connexion with this work, and that at a time when I was nearly a thousand miles absent from Bristol, and had to remain absent week after week: at such times my soul was stayed upon God; I believed His word of promise which was applicable to such cases; I poured out my soul before God, and arose from my knees in peace, because the trouble that was in the soul was in believing prayer cast upon God, and thus I was kept in peace, though I saw it to be the will of God to remain far away from the work.

"Further, when I needed houses, fellow-labourers, masters and mistresses for the Orphans or for the Day Schools, I have been enabled to look for all to the Lord and trust in Him for help.

"Dear reader, I may seem to boast; but, by the grace of God, I do not boast in thus speaking. From my inmost soul I do ascribe it to God alone that He has enabled me to trust in Him, and that hitherto He has not suffered my confidence in Him to fail. But I thought it needful to make these remarks, lest anyone should think that my depending upon God was a particular gift given to me, which other saints have no right to look for; or lest it should be thought that this my depending upon Him had *only to do with the obtaining of MONEY by prayer and faith.* By the grace of God I desire that my faith in God should extend towards EVERY thing, the smallest of my own temporal and spiritual concerns, and the smallest of the temporal and spiritual concerns of my family, towards the saints among whom I labour, the church at large, everything that has to do with the temporal and spiritual prosperity of the Scriptural Knowledge Institution, etc.

"Dear reader, do not think that I have attained in faith (and how much less in other respects!) to that degree to which I might and ought to attain; but thank God for the faith which He has given me, and ask Him to uphold and increase it. And lastly, once more, let not Satan deceive you in making you think that you could not have the same faith but that it is only for persons who are situated as I am.

"When I lose such a thing as a key, I ask the Lord to direct me to it, and I look for an answer to my prayer; when a person with whom I have made an appointment does not come, according to the fixed time, and I begin to be inconvenienced by it, I ask the Lord to be pleased to hasten him to me and I look for an answer; when I do not understand a passage of the word of God, I lift up my heart to the Lord, that He would be pleased, by His Holy Spirit to instruct me, and I expect to be taught, though I do not fix the time when, and the manner how it should be; when I am going to minister in the Word, I seek help from the Lord, and while I, in the consciousness of natural inability as well as utter unworthiness begin this His service, I am not cast down, but of good cheer, because I look for His assistance, and believe that He, for His dear Son's sake will help me. And thus in other of my temporal and spiritual concerns I pray to the Lord, and expect an answer to my requests; and may not *you* do the same, dear believing reader?

"Oh! I beseech you, do not think me an extraordinary believer, having privileges above other of God's dear children, which they cannot have; nor look on my way of acting as something that would not do for other believers. Make but trial! Do but stand still in the hour of trial, and you will see the help of God, if you trust in Him. But there is so often a forsaking the ways of the Lord in the hour of trial, and thus the *food of faith*, the means whereby our faith may be increased, is lost. This leads me to the following important point. You ask, How may I, a true believer, have my faith strengthened? The answer is this:—

"I.—Every good gift and every perfect gift is from above, and cometh down from the Father of lights, with whom is no variableness, neither shadow of turning." James i. 17. As the increase of faith is a good gift, it must come from God, and therefore He ought to be asked for this blessing.

"II.—The following means, however, ought to be used:—

"1, *The careful reading of the word of God, combined with meditation on it.* Through reading of the word of God, and especially through meditation on the word of God, the believer becomes more and more acquainted with the nature and character of God, and thus sees more and more, besides His holiness and justice, what a kind, loving, gracious, merciful, mighty, wise, and faithful Being He is, and, therefore, in poverty, affliction of body, bereavement in his family, difficulty in his service, want of a situation or employment, he will repose upon the *ability* of God to help him, because he has not only learned from His word that He is of almighty power and infinite wisdom, but he has also seen instance upon instance in the Holy Scriptures in which His almighty power and infinite wisdom have been actually exercised in helping and delivering His people; and he will repose upon the *willingness* of God to help him, because he has not only learned from the Scriptures what a kind, good, merciful, gracious, and faithful being God is, but because he has also seen in the word of God how, in a great variety of instances He has proved Himself to be so. And the consideration of this, if *God has become known to us through prayer and meditation on His own word*, will lead us, in general at least, with a measure of confidence to rely upon Him: and thus the reading of the word of God, together with meditation on it, will be one especial means to strengthen our faith.

"2, As with reference to the growth of every grace of the Spirit, it is of the utmost importance that we seek to maintain an upright heart and a good conscience, and, therefore, do not knowingly and habitually indulge in those things which are contrary to the mind of God, so it is also particularly the case with reference to the *growth in faith*. How can I possibly continue to act faith upon God, concerning anything, if I am habitually grieving Him, and seek to detract from the glory and honour of Him in whom I profess to trust, upon whom I profess to depend?

"All my confidence towards God, all my leaning upon Him in the hour of trial will be gone, if I have a guilty conscience, and do not seek to put away this guilty conscience, but still continue to do the things which are contrary to the mind of God. And if, in any particular instance, I cannot trust in God, because of the guilty conscience, then my faith is weakened by that instance of distrust; for faith with every fresh trial of it either increases by trusting God, and thus getting help, or it decreases by not trusting Him; and then there is less and less power of looking simply and directly to Him, and a habit of self-dependence is begotten or encouraged. One or the other of these will always be the case in each particular instance.

"Either we trust in God, and in that case we neither trust in ourselves, nor in our fellow-men, nor in circumstances, nor in anything besides; or we DO trust in one or more of these, and in that case do NOT trust in God.

"3, If we, indeed, desire our faith to be strengthened, we should not shrink from opportunities where our faith may be tried, and, therefore, through the trial, be strengthened.

"In our natural state we dislike dealing with God alone. Through our natural alienation from God we shrink from Him, and from eternal realities. This cleaves to us more or less, even after our regeneration. Hence it is, that more or less, even as believers, we have the same shrinking from standing with God alone,—from depending upon Him alone,—from looking to Him alone:—and yet this is the very position in which we ought to be, if we wish our faith to be strengthened. The more I am in a position to be tried in faith with reference to my body, my family, my service for the Lord, my business, etc., the more shall I have opportunity of seeing God's help and deliverance; and every fresh instance, in which He helps and delivers me, will tend towards the increase of my faith.

"On this account, therefore, the believer should not shrink from situations, positions, circumstances, in which his faith may be tried; but should cheerfully embrace them as opportunities where he may see the hand of God stretched out on his behalf, to help and deliver him, and whereby he may thus have his faith strengthened.

4, The last important point for the strengthening of our faith is, that we let God work for us, when the hour of the trial of our faith comes, and do not work a deliverance of our own. Wherever God has given faith, it is given, among other reasons, for the very purpose of being tried.

"Yea, however weak our faith may be, God will try it; only with this restriction, that as in every way, He leads on gently, gradually, patiently, so also with reference to the trial of our faith. At first our faith will be tried very little in comparison with what it may be afterwards; for God never lays more upon us that He is willing to enable us to bear. Now when the trial of faith comes, we are naturally inclined to distrust God, and to trust rather in ourselves, or in our friends, or in circumstances.

"We will rather work a deliverance of our own somehow or other, than simply look to God and wait for His help. But if we do not patiently wait for God's help, if we work a deliverance of our own, then at the next trial of our faith it will be thus again, we shall be again inclined to deliver ourselves; and thus with every fresh instance of that kind, our faith will decrease; whilst on the contrary, were we to stand still, in order to see the salvation of God, to see His hand stretched out on our behalf, trusting in Him alone, then our faith would be increased, and with every fresh case in which the hand of God is stretched out on our behalf in the hour of the trial of our faith, our faith would be increased yet more.

"Would the believer, therefore, have his faith strengthened, he must especially, *give time to God*, who tries his faith in order to prove to His child, in the end, how willing He is to help and deliver him, the moment it is good for him."

In the early years of the Institution Mr. Müller and his fellow labourers had to endure many severe trials of faith, as some of these instances show.

Mr. Müller when writing of this period says:—

"Though now (July, 1845) for about seven years our funds have been so exhausted, that it has been a *rare* case that there have been means in hand to meet the necessities of more than 100 persons for *three days* together; yet I have been only once tried in spirit, and that was on September 18, 1838, when, for the first time the Lord seemed not to regard our prayer. But when He did send help at that time, and I saw that it was only for the trial of our faith, and not because He had forsaken the work, that we were brought so low, my soul was so strengthened and encouraged, that I have not only not been allowed to distrust the Lord, but *I have not been even cast down when in the deepest poverty* since that time."

A GIFT OF £12.

"Aug. 20 [1838].—The £5 which I had received on the 18th. had been given for house-keeping, so that to-day I was again penniless. But my eyes were up to the Lord. I gave myself to prayer this morning, knowing that I should want again this week at least £13, if not above £20. To-day I received £12 in answer to prayer, from a lady who is staying at Clifton, whom I had never seen before. Adorable Lord, grant that this may be a fresh encouragement to me!"

A SOLEMN CRISIS.

Regarding one of the sharpest times of trial Mr. Müller writes:—

"Sept. 10 [1838]. Monday morning. Neither Saturday nor yesterday had any money come in. It appeared to me now needful to take some steps on account of our need, *i. e.*, to go to the Orphan-Houses, call the brethren and sisters together, (who, except brother T——, had never been informed about the state of the funds), state the case to them, see how much money was needed for the present, tell them that amidst all this trial of faith I still believed that God would help, and to pray with them.

"Especially, also, I meant to go for the sake of telling them that no more articles must be purchased than we have the means to pay for, but to let there be nothing lacking in any way to the children as it regards nourishing food and needful clothing; for I would rather at once send them away than that they should lack. I meant to go for the sake also of seeing whether there were still articles remaining which had been sent for the purpose of being sold, or whether there were any articles really needless, that we might turn them into money. I felt that the matter was now come to a solemn crisis. About half-past nine sixpence came in, which had been put anonymously into the box at Gideon Chapel. This money seemed to me like an earnest, that God would have compassion and send more.

About ten, after I had returned from brother Craik, to whom I had unbosomed my heart again, whilst once more in prayer for help, a sister called who gave two sovereigns to my wife for the Orphans, stating that she had felt herself stirred up to come and that she had delayed coming already too long. A few minutes after, when I went into the room where she was, she gave me two sovereigns more, and all this without knowing the least about our need. Thus the Lord most mercifully has sent us a little help, to the great encouragement of my faith. A few minutes after I was called on for money from the Infant Orphan-House, to which I sent £2, and £1 0s. 6d. to the Boys' Orphan-House, and £1 to the Girls' Orphan-House."

A PRECIOUS DELIVERANCE.

"Sept. 17 [1838].—The trial still continues. It is now more and more trying, even to faith, as each day comes. Truly, the Lord has wise purposes in allowing us to call so long upon Him for help. But I am sure God will send help, if we can but wait. One of the labourers had had a little money come in of which he gave 12s. 6d.; another labourer gave 11s. 8d., being all the money she had left; this, with 17s. 6d., which, partly, had come in, and, partly was in hand, enabled us to pay what needed to be paid, and to purchase provisions, so that nothing yet, in any way, has been lacking. This evening I was rather tired respecting the long delay of larger sums coming; but being led to go to the Scriptures for comfort, my soul was greatly refreshed, and my faith again strengthened, by the xxxivth Psalm, so that I went very cheerfully to meet with my dear fellow-labourers for prayer. I read to them the Psalm, and sought to cheer their hearts through the precious promises contained in it."

"Sept. 18.—Brother T. had 25s. in hand, and I had 3s. This £1 8s. enabled us to buy the meat and bread, which was needed; a little tea for one of the houses, and milk for all; no more than this is needed. Thus the Lord has provided not only for this day; for there is bread for two days in hand. Now, however, we are come to an extremity. The funds are exhausted. The labourers, who had a little money, have given as long as they had any left.

"Now observe how the Lord helped us! A lady from the neighbourhood of London who brought a parcel with money from her daughter, arrived four or five days since in Bristol, and took lodgings next door to the Boys' Orphan-House. This afternoon she herself kindly brought me the money, amounting to £3 2s. 6d. We had been reduced so low as to be on the point of selling those things which could be spared; but this morning I had asked the Lord, if it might be, to prevent the necessity, of our doing so. That the money had been so near the Orphan-Houses for several days without being given, is a plain proof that it was from the beginning in the heart of God to help us; but because He delights in the prayers of His children, He had allowed us to pray so long; also to try our faith, and to make the answer so much the sweeter. It is indeed a precious deliverance. I burst out into loud praises and thanks the first moment I was alone, after I had received the money. I met with my fellow-labourers again this evening for prayer and praise; their hearts were not a little cheered. This money was this evening divided, and will comfortably provide for all that will be needed tomorrow."

CHAPTER II
THE NEW ORPHAN HOUSES, ASHLEY DOWN.

A COMPLAINT having been received from a gentleman in October, 1845, that some of the inhabitants of Wilson Street were inconvenienced by the Orphan-Houses being in that street, Mr. Müller ultimately decided for that and other reasons, after much prayerful meditation, to build an Orphan-House elsewhere to accommodate 300 children, and commenced to ask the Lord for means for so doing:—

"Jan. 31 [1846].—It is now 89 days since I have been daily waiting upon God about the building of an Orphan-House. The time seems to me now near when the Lord will give us a piece of ground, and I told the brethren and sisters so this evening, after our usual Saturday evening prayer meeting at the Orphan-Houses.

"Feb. 1.—A poor widow sent to-day 10s.

"Feb. 2.—Today I heard of suitable and cheap land on Ashley Down.

"Feb. 3.—Saw the land. It is the most desirable of all I have seen.

"—There was anonymously put in an Orphan-box at my house a sovereign, in a piece of paper, on which was written, 'The New Orphan-House.'

"Feb. 4.—This evening I called on the owner of the land on Ashley Down, about which I had heard on the 2nd, but he was not at home. As I, however, had been informed that I should find him at his house of business, I went there, but did not find him there either, as he had *just before* left. I might have called again at his residence, at a later hour having been informed by one of the servants that he would be sure to be at home about eight o'clock; but I did not do so, judging that there was the hand of God in my not finding him at either place: and I judged it best therefore not to force the matter, but to 'let patience have her perfect work.'

"Feb. 5.—Saw this morning the owner of the land. He told me that he awoke at three o'clock this morning and could not sleep again till five. While he was thus lying awake, his mind was all the time occupied about the piece of land, respecting which inquiry had been made of him for the building of an Orphan-House, at my request; and he determined that if I should apply for it, he would not only let me have it, but for £120 per acre, instead of £200; the price which he had previously asked for it. How good is the Lord! The agreement was made this morning, and I purchased a field of nearly seven acres, at £120 per acre.

"Observe the hand of God in my not finding the owner at home last evening! The Lord meant to speak to His servant first about this matter, during a sleepless night, and to lead him *fully* to decide, before I had seen him."

"BECAUSE OF HIS IMPORTUNITY."

"Nov. 19 [1846].—I am now led more and more to importune the Lord to send me the means, which are requisite in order that I may be able to commence the building. Because:

1. it has been for some time past publicly stated in print, that I allow it is not without ground that some of the inhabitants of Wilson Street consider themselves inconvenienced by the Orphan-Houses being in that street, and I long therefore to be able to remove the Orphans from thence as soon as possible.

2. I become more and more convinced, that it would be greatly for the benefit of the children, both physically and morally, with God's blessing, to be in

such a position as they are intended to occupy, when the New Orphan-House shall have been built. And

3. because the number of very poor and destitute Orphans, that are waiting for admission, is so great, and there are constantly fresh applications made. Now whilst, by God's grace, I would not wish the building to be begun one single day sooner than is His will; and whilst I firmly believe, that He will give me, in His own time every shilling which I need; yet I also know, that He delights in being earnestly entreated, and that He takes pleasure in the continuance in prayer, and in the importuning Him, which so clearly is to be seen from the parable of the widow and the unjust judge, Luke xviii. 1-8.

"For these reasons I gave myself again particularly to prayer last evening, that the Lord would send further means, being also especially led to do so, in addition to the above reasons, because there had come in but little comparatively, since the 29th of last month. This morning, between five and six o'clock I prayed again, among other points, about the Building Fund, and then had a long season for the reading of the word of God. In the course of my reading I came to Mark xi. 24, 'What things soever ye desire, when ye pray, believe that ye receive them, and ye shall have them.'

"The importance of the truth contained in this portion I have often felt and spoken about; but this morning I felt it again most particularly, and, applying it to the New Orphan-House, said to the Lord: 'Lord I believe that Thou wilt give me all I need for this work. I am sure that I shall have all, because I believe that I receive in answer to my prayer.' Thus, with the heart full of peace concerning this work, I went on to the other part of the chapter, and to the next chapter.

"After family prayer I had again my usual season for

prayer with regard to all the many parts of the work, and the various necessities thereof, asking also blessings upon my fellow-labourers, upon the circulation of Bibles and Tracts, and upon the precious souls in the Adult School, the Sunday Schools, the Six Day Schools, and the four Orphan-Houses.

"Amidst all the many things I again made my requests about means for the Building. And now observe: About five minutes, after I had risen from my knees, there was given to me a registered letter, containing a cheque for £300, of which £280 are for the Building Fund, £10 for my own personal expenses, and £10 for Brother Craik. The Lord's holy name be praised for this precious encouragement, by which the Building Fund is now increased to more than six thousand pounds."

MR. MÜLLER'S FIRST ORPHAN-HOUSE.

"Jan. 25 [1847].—The season of the year is now approaching, when building may be begun. Therefore with increased earnestness I have given myself unto prayer, importuning the Lord that He would be pleased to appear on our behalf, and speedily send the remainder of the amount which is required, and I have increasingly, of late, felt that the time is drawing near, when the Lord will give me all that which is requisite for commencing the building.

"All the various arguments which I have often brought before God, I brought also again this morning before Him. It is now 14 months and 3 weeks since day by day I have uttered my petitions to God on behalf of this work. I rose from my knees this morning in full confidence, not only that God *could*, but also *would*, send the means, and that soon. Never, during all these 14 months and 3 weeks, have I had the least doubt, that I should have all that which is requisite.—And now, dear believing reader, rejoice and praise with me.

"About an hour, after I had prayed thus, there was

given to me the sum of Two Thousand Pounds for the Building Fund. Thus I have received altogether £9,285 3s. 9½d. towards this work.—I cannot describe the joy I had in God when I received this donation. It must be known from experience, in order to be felt. 447 days I have had day by day to wait upon God, before the sum reached the above amount. How great is the blessing which the soul obtains by *trusting in God*, and *by waiting patiently*. Is it not manifest how precious it is to carry on God's work in this way, even with regard to the obtaining of means?"

The total amount which came in for the Building Fund was £15,784 18s. 10d.

ORPHAN-HOUSES NOS. 2 & 3.

"March 12, 1862.—It was in November, 1850, that my mind became exercised about enlarging the Orphan Work from 300 Orphans to 1000, and subsequently to 1150; and it was in June, 1851, that this my purpose became known, having kept it secret for more than seven months, whilst day by day praying about it. From the end of November, 1850, to this day, March 12, 1862, not one single day has been allowed to pass, without this contemplated enlargement being brought before God in prayer, and generally more than once a day. But only now, this day, the New Orphan-House No. 3 was so far advanced, that it could be opened. Observe then, first, esteemed Reader, how long it may be, before a full answer to our prayers, even to thousands and tens of thousands of prayers, is granted; yea, though those prayers may be believing prayers, earnest prayers, and offered up in the name of the Lord Jesus, and though we may only for the sake of the honour of our Lord desire the answer: for I did, by the grace of God, without the least doubt and wavering look for more than eleven years for the full answer; and I sought only in this matter the glory of God."

PRAYING THREE TIMES DAILY FOR HELPERS.

"As in the case of No. 2, so also in the case of the New Orphan-House No. 3, I had daily prayed for the needed helpers and assistants for the various departments. Before a stone was laid, I began to pray for this; and, as the building progressed, I continued day by day to bring this matter before God, feeling assured, that, as in everything else, so in this particular also, He would graciously be pleased to appear on our behalf and help us, as the whole work is intended for His honour and glory.

"At last the time was near when the house could be opened, and the time therefore near when the applications, which had been made in writing during more than two years previously, should be considered, for the filling up of the various posts. It now, however, was found that, whilst there had been about 50 applications made for the various situations, some places could not be filled up, because either the individuals, who had applied for them, were married, or were, on examination, found unsuitable.

"This was no small trial of faith; for day by day, for years, had I asked God to help me in this particular, even as He had done in the case of the New Orphan-House No. 2; I had also expected help, confidently expected help: and yet now, when help *seemed* needed, it was wanting. What was now to be done, dear Reader? Would it have been right to charge God with unfaithfulness?

"Would it have been right to distrust Him? Would it have been right to say, it is useless to pray? By no means. This, on the contrary, I did; I thanked God for all the help, He had given me in connection with the whole of the enlargement; I thanked Him for enabling me to overcome so many and such great difficulties; I thanked Him for the helpers He had given me for No. 2; I thanked Him, also, for the helpers He had given me already for No. 3; and instead of distrusting God, I looked upon this delay of the full answer to prayer, only as a trial of faith, and therefore resolved, that, instead of praying *once* a day with my dear wife about this matter, as we had been doing day by day for years, we should now meet daily *three* times, to bring this before God.

"I also brought the matter before the whole staff of my helpers in the work requesting their prayers. Thus I have now continued for about four months longer in prayer, day by day calling upon God three times on account of this need, and the result has been, that one helper after the other has been given, without the help coming *too* late, or the work getting into confusion; or the reception of the children being hindered; and I am fully assured, that the few who are yet needed will also be found, when they are *really* required."

DIFFICULTIES REMOVED AFTER PRAYER AND PATIENCE.

Mr. Müller relates the following incidents in connection with the purchase of the land for the Fourth and Fifth Orphan-Houses, after receiving five thousand pounds for the Building Fund:

"I had now, through all that had come in since May 26th, 1864, including this last-mentioned donation, above Twenty-Seven Thousand Pounds in hand. I had patiently waited God's time. I had determined to do nothing, until I had the full half of the sum needed for the two houses. But now, having above Two Thousand Pounds beyond the half, I felt, after again seeking counsel from God, quite happy, in taking steps for the purchase of land.

"My eyes had been for years directed to a beautiful piece of land, only separated by the turnpike road from the ground on which the New Orphan-House No. 3 is erected. The land is about 18 acres, with a small house and outhouses built on one end thereof. Hundreds of times had I prayed, within the last years, that God for Jesus' sake would count me worthy, to be allowed to erect on this ground two more Orphan-Houses; and hundreds of times I had with a prayerful eye looked on this land, yea, as it were, bedewed it with my prayers. I might have bought it years ago; but that would have been going before the Lord.

"I had money enough in hand to have paid for it years ago; but I desired patiently, submissively, to wait God's own time, and for Him to mark it clearly and distinctly that His time was come, and that I took the step according to His will; for whatever I might apparently accomplish, if the work were mine, and not the Lord's, I could expect no blessing. But now the Lord's mind was clearly and distinctly made manifest.

"I had enough money in hand to pay for the land and to build one house, and therefore I went forward, after having still asked the Lord for guidance, and being assured that it was His will I should take active steps. The first thing I did was, to see the agent who acted for the owner of the land, and to ask him, whether the land was for sale. He replied that it was, but that it was let till March 25th, 1867. He said that he would write for the price.

"Here a great difficulty at once presented itself, that the land was let for two years and four months longer, whilst it appeared desirable that I should be able to take possession of it in about six months, viz., as soon as the conveyance could be made out, and the plans be ready for the New Orphan-House No. 4, and arrangements be made with contractors. But I was not discouraged by this difficulty; for I expected, through prayer, to make happy and satisfactory arrangements with the tenant, being willing to give him a fair compensation for leaving before his time had expired.

"But, before I had time to see about this, two other great difficulties presented themselves: the one was, that the owner asked £7,000 for the land, which I judged to be considerably more than its value; and the other, that I heard that the Bristol Waterworks Company intended to make an additional reservoir for their water, on this very land, and to get an Act of Parliament passed to that effect.

"Pause here for a few moments, esteemed Reader. You have seen, how the Lord brought me so far, with regard to pecuniary means, that I felt now warranted to go forward; and I may further add, that I was brought to this point as the result of thousands of times praying regarding this object; and that there were, also, many hundreds of children waiting for admission; and yet, after the Lord Himself so manifestly had appeared on our behalf, by the donation of £5,000, He allows this apparent death-blow to come upon the whole.

"But thus I have found it hundreds of times since I have known the Lord. The difficulties, which He is pleased to allow to arise, are only allowed, under such circumstances, for the exercise of our faith and patience; and more prayer, more patience, and the exercise of faith, will remove the difficulties.

"Now, as I knew the Lord, these difficulties were no insurmountable difficulties to me, for I put my trust in Him, according to that word: "The Lord also will be a refuge for the oppressed, a refuge in times of trouble. And they that know Thy name will put their trust in Thee: for Thou, Lord, hast not forsaken them that seek Thee." (Psalm ix. 9, 10).

"I gave myself, therefore, earnestly to prayer concerning all these three especial difficulties which had arisen regarding the land. I prayed several times daily about the matter, and used the following means:

"1. I saw the Acting Committee of the Directors of the Bristol Waterworks Company regarding their intended reservoir on the land, which I was about to purchase, and stated to them, what I had seen in print concerning their intentions. They courteously stated to me, that only a small portion of the land would be required, not enough to interfere with my purpose; and that, if it could be avoided, even this small portion should not be taken.

"2. This being settled, I now saw the tenant, after many prayers; for I desired, as a Christian, that if this land were bought, it should be done under amicable circumstances with regard to him. At the first interview, I stated my intentions to him, at the same time expressing my desire that the matter should be settled pleasantly with regard to himself. He said that he would consider the matter, and desired a few days for that purpose.

"After a week I saw him again, and he then kindly stated, that, as the land was wanted for such an object, he would not stand in the way; but that, as he had laid out a good deal on the house and land, he expected a compensation for leaving it before his time was up. As I, of course, was quite willing to give a *fair* and *reasonable* compensation, I considered this a very precious answer to prayer.

"3. I now entered upon the third difficulty, the price of the land. I knew well how much the land was worth to the Orphan Institution; but its value to the Institution was not the market value. I gave myself, therefore, day by day to prayer, that the Lord would constrain the owner to accept a considerably lower sum than he had asked; I also pointed out to him why it was not worth as much as he asked.

"At last he consented to take £5,500 instead of £7,000, and I accepted the offer; for I knew that by the level character of the land we should save a considerable sum for the two houses, and that by the new sewer, which only a few months before had been completed, running along under the turnpike road near the field, we should be considerably benefited. In addition to these two points I had to take into the account, that we can have gas from Bristol, as in the three houses already in operation.

"And lastly, the most important point of all, the nearness of this piece of land to the other three houses, so that all could easily be under the same direction and superintendence. In fact, no other piece of land, near or far off, would present so much advantage to us, as this spot, which the Lord thus so very kindly had given to us. All being now settled, I proceeded to have the land conveyed to the same trustees who stood trustees for the New Orphan-Houses No. 1, No. 2, and No. 3.—I have thus minutely dwelt on these various matters for the encouragement of the reader, that he may not be discouraged by difficulties, however great and many and varied, but give himself to prayer, trusting in the Lord for help, yea, expecting help, which, in His own time and way, He will surely grant."

ORPHAN-HOUSES NOS. 4 & 5.

"March 5, 1874.—Both houses, No. 4 and No. 5, have now been for years in operation, No. 4 since Nov. 1868 and No. 5 since the beginning of the year 1870, and above 1,200 Orphans have been already received into them, and month after month more are received, as the Orphans are sent out from them as apprentices or servants. Moreover all the expenses in connection with their being built, fitted up and furnished were met to the full, as the demands arose, and, after all had been paid, there was left a balance of several thousand pounds, which is being used for keeping the houses in repair.

"See, esteemed Reader, how abundantly God answered our prayers, and how plain it is, that we were not mistaken, after we had patiently and prayerfully sought to ascertain His will. Be encouraged, therefore, yet further and further to confide in the Living God."

CHAPTER III
PRECIOUS ANSWERS TO PRAYER

IN REMARKABLE WAYS God helped Mr. Müller as "The Narratives" show:—

THE ARTIST'S FIRST RETURN.

"April 30 [1859].—Received the following letter from a considerable distance: 'My dear Christian Brother, I am the husband of Mrs. —— who sends you by this post the two Sovereign piece. How can we better dispose of this relic of affectionate remembrance, than by depositing it in the bank of Christ, who always pays the best interest, and never fails.—Now, my best and spiritual counsellor, I cannot express to you the exceeding great joy I feel, in relating what follows. I am an artist, a *poor* artist, a landscape painter.

"About two weeks ago I sent a picture to Bristol for exhibition, just as I finished your book that was lent us. I most humbly and earnestly prayed to God to enable me, by the sale of my Bristol picture, to have the blessed privilege of sending you *half the proceeds*. The price of the picture is £20. Now mark. Immediately the exhibition is open, God, in His mercy, mindful of my prayer, sends me a purchaser. I have exhibited in Bristol before, *but never sold* a picture. Oh! my dear friend, my very heart leaps for joy. I have never been so near God before.

"Through your instrumentality I have been enabled to draw nearer to God, with more earnestness, more faith, more holy desires.—This is the *first return* God has blessed me with for the whole of my last year's labours. What a blessing to have it so returned!—Oh, with what joy I read your book!—The picture I speak of is now being exhibited in the academy of arts at Clifton, numbered in the Catalogue ——, the title is ——. I cannot pay you till the close of the exhibition, as

I shall not be paid till then, &c.' Of such letters I have had thousands during the last 40 years."

THE NORTH WIND CHANGED INTO A SOUTH WIND.

"It was towards the end of November of 1857, when I was most unexpectedly informed that the boiler of our heating apparatus at No. 1 leaked very considerably, so that it was impossible to go through the winter with such a leak.—Our heating apparatus consists of a large cylinder boiler, inside of which the fire is kept, and with which boiler the water pipes, that warm the rooms, are connected. Hot air is also connected with this apparatus. The boiler had been considered suited for the work of the winter. To suspect that it was worn out, and not to do anything towards replacing it by a new one, and to have said, I will trust in God regarding it, would be careless presumption, but not faith in God. It would be the counterfeit of faith.

"The boiler is entirely surrounded by brickwork; its state, therefore, could not be known without taking down the brickwork; this, if needless, would be rather injurious to the boiler, than otherwise; and as for eight winters we had had no difficulty in this way, we had not anticipated it now. But suddenly, and most unexpectedly, at the commencement of the winter, this difficulty occurred. What then was to be done? For the children, especially the younger infants, I felt deeply concerned, that they might not suffer, through want of warmth. But how were we to obtain warmth?

"The introduction of a *new* boiler would, in all probability, take many weeks. The *repairing* of the boiler was a questionable matter, on account of the greatness of the leak; but, if not, nothing could be said of it, till the brick-chamber in which it is enclosed, was, at least in part, removed; but that would, at least, as far as we could judge, take days; and what was to be done in the meantime, to find warm rooms for 300 children? It naturally occurred to me, to introduce temporary gas-stoves; but on further weighing the matter, it was found, that we should be unable to heat our very large rooms with gas, except we had many stoves, which we could not introduce, as we had not a sufficient quantity of gas to spare from our lighting apparatus. Moreover, for each of these stoves we needed a small chimney, to carry off the impure air. This mode of heating, therefore, though applicable to a hall, a staircase, or a shop, would not suit our purpose.

"I also thought of the temporary introduction of Arnott's stoves; but they would have been unsuitable, requiring long chimneys (as they would have been of a temporary kind) to go out of the windows. On this account, the uncertainty of their answering in our case, and the disfigurement of the rooms, led me to give up this plan also. But what was to be done? Gladly would I have paid £100, if thereby the difficulty could have been overcome, and the children not be exposed to suffer for many days from being in cold rooms. At last I determined on falling entirely into the hands of God, who is very merciful and of tender compassion, and I decided on having the brick-chamber opened, to see the extent of the damage, and whether the boiler might be repaired, so as to carry us through the winter.

"The day was fixed, when the workmen were to come, and all the necessary arrangements were made. The fire, of course, had to be let out while the repairs were going on. But now see. After the day was fixed for the repairs a bleak North wind set in. It began to blow either on Thursday or Friday before the Wednesday afternoon, when the fire was to be let out. Now came the first really cold weather, which we had in the beginning of that winter, during the first days of December.

"What was to be done? The repairs could not be put off. I now asked the Lord for two things, viz., that He would be pleased to change the north wind into a south wind, and that He would give to the workmen 'a mind to work'; for I remembered how much Nehemiah accomplished in 52 days, whilst building the walls of Jerusalem, because 'the people had a mind to work.' Well, the memorable day came.

"The evening before, the bleak north wind blew still: but, on the Wednesday, the south wind blew: exactly as I had prayed. The weather was so mild that no fire was needed. The brickwork is removed, the leak is found out very soon, the boiler makers begin to repair in good earnest. About half-past eight in the evening, when I was going home, I was informed at the lodge, that the acting principal of the firm, whence the boiler makers came, had arrived to see how the work was going on, and whether he could in any way speed the matter. I went immediately, therefore, into the cellar, to see him with the men, to seek to expedite the business. In speaking to the principal of this, he said in their hearing, 'the men will work late this evening, and come very early again tomorrow.'

"'We would rather, Sir,' said the leader, 'work all night.' Then remembered I the second part of my prayer, that God would give the men 'a mind to work.' Thus it was: by the morning the repair was accomplished, the leak was stopped, though with great difficulty, and within about 30 hours the brickwork was up again, and the fire in the boiler; and all the time the south wind blew so mildly, that there was not the least need of a fire.

"Here, then, is one of our difficulties which was overcome by prayer and faith."

CONVERSION OF THE ORPHANS.

"May 26, 1860.—Day after day, and year after year, by the help of God, we labour in prayer for the spiritual benefit of the Orphans under our care. These our supplications, which have been for 24 years brought before the Lord concerning them, have been abundantly answered, in former years, in the conversion of hundreds from among them. We have, also, had repeated seasons in which, within a short time, or even all at once, *many* of the Orphans were converted.

"Such a season we had about three years since, when, within a few days, about 60 were brought to believe in the Lord Jesus; and such seasons we have had again twice during the first year. The first was in July, 1859, when the Spirit of God wrought so mightily in one school of 120 girls, as that very many, yea more than one-half, were brought under deep concern about the salvation of their souls.

"This work, moreover, was not a mere momentary excitement; but, after more than eleven months have elapsed, there are 31 concerning whom there is *full* confidence as to their conversion, and 32 concerning whom there is likewise a goodly measure of confidence, though not to the same amount, as regarding the 31.

"There are therefore 63 out of the 120 Orphans in that one School who are considered to have been converted in July, 1859. This blessed and mighty work of the Holy Spirit cannot be traced to any particular cause. It was however, a most precious answer to prayer. As such we look upon it, and are encouraged by it to further waiting upon God.

"The second season of the mighty working of the Holy Spirit among the Orphans, during the past year, was at the end of January and the beginning of February, 1860. The particulars of it are of the deepest interest; but I must content myself by stating, that this great work of the Spirit of God in January and February, 1860, began among the younger class of the children under our care, little girls of about 6, 7, 8 and 9 years old; then extended to the older girls; and then to the boys, so that within about 10 days above 200 of the Orphans were stirred up to be anxious about their souls, and in *many* instances found peace *immediately*, through faith in our Lord Jesus. They at once requested to be allowed to hold prayer-meetings among themselves, and have had these meetings ever since. Many of them also manifested a concern about the salvation of their companions and relations, and spoke or wrote to them, about the way to be saved."

APPRENTICING THE ORPHANS.

"In the early part of the summer, 1862, it was found that we had several boys ready to be apprenticed; but there were no applications made by masters for apprentices. As all our boys are invariably sent out as indoor apprentices, this was no small difficulty; for we not only look for Christian masters, but consider their business, and examine into their position, to see whether they are suitable; and the master must also be willing to receive the apprentice into his own family. Under these circumstances, we again gave ourselves to prayer, as we had done for more than twenty years before, concerning this thing, instead of advertising, which, in all probability, would only bring before us masters who desire apprentices for the sake of the premium.

"We remembered how good the Lord had been to us, in having helped us hundreds of times before, in this very matter. Some weeks passed, but the difficulty remained. We continued, however, in prayer, and then one application was made, and then another; and since we first began to pray about this matter, last summer, we have been able to send out altogether 18 boys up to May 26, 1863; the difficulty was thus again entirely overcome by prayer, as every one of the boys, whom it was desirable to send out, has been sent out."

SICKNESS AT THE ORPHANAGE.

Sickness at times visited the houses.

"During the summer and autumn of 1866 we had also the measles at all the three Orphan-Houses. After they had made their appearance, our especial prayer was:

"1. That there might not be too many children ill at one time in this disease, so that our accommodation in the Infirmary rooms or otherwise might be sufficient. This prayer was answered to the full; for though we had at the New Orphan-House No. 1 not less than 83 cases, in No. 2 altogether 111, and in No. 3 altogether 68; yet God so graciously was pleased to listen to our supplications, as that when our spare rooms were filled with the invalids, He so long stayed the spreading of the measles till a sufficient number were restored, so as to make room for others, who were taken ill.

"2. Further we prayed, that the children, who were taken ill in the measles, might be safely brought through and not die. Thus it was. We had the full answer to our prayers; for though 262 children altogether had the measles, not one of them died.

"3. Lastly we prayed, that no evil physical consequences might follow this disease, as is so often the case; this was also granted. All the 262 children not only recovered, but did well afterwards. I gratefully record this signal mercy and blessing of God, and this full and precious answer to prayer, to the honour of His name."

HELP FOR NEEDY BRETHREN.

"1863.—"The end of the year was now at hand, and, in winding up the accounts, it was my earnest desire, to do once more all I could, in sending help to needy labourers in the gospel. I went therefore through the list, writing against the various names of those to whom I had not already recently sent, what amount it appeared desirable to send; and I found, when these sums were added together, the total was £476, but £280 was all I had in hand. I wrote therefore a cheque for £280, though I would have gladly sent £476, yet felt thankful, at the same time, that I had this amount in hand for these brethren.

"Having written the cheque, as the last occupation of the day, then came my usual season for prayer, for the many things which I daily, by the help of God, bring before Him; and then again, I brought also the case of these preachers of the Gospel before the Lord, and besought Him that He would even now be pleased to give me yet a goodly sum for them, though there remained but three days to the close of our year. This being done, I went home about nine o'clock in the evening, and found there had arrived from a great distance £100 for Missions, with £100 left at my disposal, and £5 for myself. I took, therefore, the whole £200 for Missions, and thus had £480 in hand to meet the £476 which I desired for this object.

"Those who know the blessedness of really trusting in God, and getting help from Him, as in this case, in answer to prayer, will be able to enter into the spiritual enjoyment I had in the reception of that donation, in which both the answer to prayer was granted, and with it the great enjoyment of gladdening the hearts of many devoted servants of Christ."

THE HEART'S DESIRE GIVEN TO HELP MISSION WORK IN CHINA.

"Sept. 30 [1869].—From Yorkshire £50.—Received also One Thousand Pounds today for the Lord's work in China. About this donation it is especially to be noticed, that for months it had been my earnest desire to do more than ever for Mission Work in China, and I had already taken steps to carry out this desire, when this donation of One Thousand Pounds came to hand.

"This precious answer to prayer for means should be a particular encouragement to all who are engaged in the Lord's work, and who may need means for it. It proves afresh, that, if our work is His work, and we honour Him, by waiting upon and looking to Him for means, He will surely, in His own time and way, supply them."

THE JOY OF ANSWERS TO PRAYER.

"The joy which answers to prayer give, cannot be described; and the impetus which they afford to the spiritual life is exceedingly great. The experience of this happiness I desire for all my Christian readers. If you believe indeed in the Lord Jesus for the salvation of your soul, if you walk uprightly and do not regard iniquity in your heart, if you continue to wait patiently, and believingly upon God; then answers will surely be given to your prayers. You may not be called upon to serve the Lord in the way the writer does, and therefore may never have answers to prayer respecting such things as are recorded here; but, in your various circumstances, your family, your business, your profession, your church position, your labour for the Lord, etc., you may have answers as distinct as any here recorded."

THE GREAT NEED OF BEING SAVED BY FAITH IN CHRIST JESUS.

"Should this, however, be read by any who are not believers in the Lord Jesus, but who are going on in the carelessness or self-righteousness of their unrenewed hearts, then I would affectionately and solemnly beseech such, first of all to be reconciled to God by faith in the Lord Jesus. You are sinners. You deserve punishment. If you do not see this, ask God to show it unto you.

"Let this now be your first and especial prayer. Ask God also to enlighten you not merely concerning your state by nature, but especially to reveal the Lord Jesus to your heart. God sent Him, that He might bear the punishment, due to us guilty sinners.

"God accepts the obedience and sufferings of the Lord Jesus, in the room of those who depend upon Him for the salvation of their souls; and the moment a sinner believes in the Lord Jesus, he obtains the forgiveness of all his sins. When thus he is reconciled to God, by faith in the Lord Jesus, and has obtained the forgiveness of his sins, he has boldness to enter into the presence of God, to make known his requests unto Him; and the more he is enabled to realise that his sins are forgiven, and that God, for Christ's sake, is well pleased with those who believe on Him, the more ready he will be to come with all his wants, both temporal and spiritual, to his Heavenly Father, that He may supply them. But as long as the consciousness of unpardoned guilt remains, so long shall we be kept at a distance from God, especially as it regards prayer. Therefore, dear reader, if you are an unforgiven sinner, let your first and especial prayer be, that God would be pleased to reveal to your heart the Lord Jesus, His beloved Son."

A DOUBLE ANSWER.

"July 25 [1865].—From the neighbourhood of London £100, with the following letter: 'My dear Sir, I believe that it is through the Lord's actings upon me, that I enclose you a cheque on the Bank of England, Western Branch, for £100. I hope that your affairs are going on well. Yours in the Lord —-.'

"This Christian gentleman, whom I have never seen, and who is engaged in a very large business in London, had sent me several times before a similar sum. A day or two before I received this last kind donation, I had asked the Lord, that He would be pleased to influence the heart of this donor to help me again, which I had never done before regarding him; and thus I had the double answer to prayer, in that not only money came in, but money from *him*.

"The reader will now see the meaning in the donor's letter, when he wrote 'I believe that it is through the Lord's actings upon me that I enclose you a cheque, &c.' Verily it was the Lord who acted upon this gentleman, to send me this sum. Perhaps the reader may think, that in acknowledging the receipt of the donation, I wrote to the donor what I have here stated. I did not. My reason for not doing so was, lest he should have thought I was in especial need, and might have been thus influenced to send more.

"In truly knowing the Lord, in really relying upon Him and upon Him alone, there is no need of giving hints directly or indirectly, whereby individuals may be induced further to help. I might have written to the donor (as was indeed the case), I need a considerable sum day by day for the current expenses of the various objects of the Institution, and also might have with truth told him, at that time, that I yet needed about Twenty Thousand Pounds, to enable me to meet all the expenses connected with the contemplated enlargement of the Orphan work. But my practice is, never to allude to any of these things in my correspondence with donors. When the Report is published, every one can see, who has a desire to see, how matters stand; and thus I leave things in the hands of God, to speak for us to the hearts of His stewards. And this He does. Verily we do not wait upon God in vain!"

CHRISTIANS IN BUSINESS.

"Jan. 1 [1869].—From Scotland £50 for Missions, £25 for the circulation of the Holy Scriptures and £25 for the circulation of Tracts. Received also from a considerable distance £10 for these objects, with £10 for the Orphans.

"About this latter donation I make a few remarks. At the early part of the year 1868, a Christian business man wrote to me for advice in his peculiar difficult business affairs. His letter showed that he had a desire to walk in the ways of the Lord, and to carry on his business to the glory of God; but his circumstances were of the most trying character. I therefore wrote to him to come to Bristol, that I might be able to advise him. Accordingly he undertook the long journey, and I had an interview with him, through which I saw his most trying position in business.

"Having fully conversed with him, I gave him the following counsel:

"1, That he should day by day, expressly for the purpose, retire with his Christian wife, that they might unitedly spread their business difficulties before God in prayer, and do this, if possible, twice a day.

"2, That he should look out for answers to his prayers, and expect that God would help him.

"3, That he should avoid all business trickeries, such as exposing for sale two or three articles, marked below cost price, for the sake of attracting customers, because of its being unbecoming a disciple of the Lord Jesus to use such artifices; and that, if he did so, he could not reckon on the blessing of God.

"4, I advised him further, to set apart; out of his profits, week by week, a certain proportion for the work of God, whether his income was much or little, and use this income faithfully for the Lord.

"5, Lastly, I asked him, to let me know, month after month, how the Lord dealt with him.

"—The reader will feel interested to learn, that from that time the Lord was pleased to prosper the business of this dear Christian brother, so that his returns from the 1st of March, 1868, up to March 1, 1869, were £9,138 13s. 5d., while during the same period the previous year they had been only £6,609 18s. 3d., therefore £2,528 15s. 2d. more than the year before.

"When he sent me the donation above referred to, he also writes, that he had been enabled to put aside during the previous year £123 13s. 3d. for the work of God or the need of the poor.—I have so fully dwelt on this, because Christians in business may be benefited by it."

REVIVAL IN THE ORPHAN-HOUSES.

"In giving the statistics of the previous year [1871-72], I referred already to the great spiritual blessing, which it pleased the Lord to grant to the Orphan Work at the end of that year and the beginning of this; but, as this is so deeply important a subject, I enter somewhat further and more fully into it here. It was stated before, that the spiritual condition of the Orphans generally gave to us great sorrow of heart, because there were so few, comparatively, among them, who were in earnest about their souls, and resting on the atoning death of the Lord Jesus for salvation. This our sorrow led us to lay it on the whole staff of assistants, matrons and teachers, to seek earnestly the Lord's blessing on the souls of the children. This was done in our united prayer meetings, and, I have reason to believe, in secret also; and in answer to these our secret and united prayers, in the year 1872, there were, as the result of this, more believers by far among the Orphans than ever.

"On Jan. 8, 1872, the Lord began to work among them, and this work was going on more or less afterwards. In the New Orphan-House No. 3, it showed itself least, till it pleased the Lord to lay His hand heavily on that house, by the small-pox; and, from that time the working of the Holy Spirit was felt in that house also, particularly in one department.

"At the end of July, 1872, I received the statements of all the matrons and teachers in the five houses, who reported to me, that, after careful observation and conversation, they had good reason to believe that 729 of the Orphans then under our care, were believers in the Lord Jesus. This number of believing Orphans is by far greater than ever we had, for which we adore and praise the Lord! See how the Lord overruled the great trial, occasioned by the small-pox, and turned it into a great blessing! See, also, how, after so low a state, comparatively, which led us to prayer, earnest prayer, the working of the Holy Spirit was more manifest than ever!"

MR. MÜLLER'S MISSION TOURS.

In the year 1875, when seventy years of age, Mr. Müller was led to start on his Missionary Tours, and during the next twenty years preached to more than three million people, in forty-two countries of the world.

"On August 8th, 1882," Mr. Müller says, "we began our ninth Missionary Tour. The first place at which I preached was Weymouth, where I spoke in public four times. From Weymouth we went, by way of Calais and Brussels, to Düsseldorf on the Rhine, where I preached many times six years before.

"During this visit, I spoke there in public eight times. Regarding my stay at Düsseldorf, for the encouragement of the reader, I relate the following circumstance. During our first visit to that city, in the year 1876, a godly City Missionary came to me one day, greatly tried, because he had six sons, for whose conversion he had been praying many years, and yet they remained unconcerned about their souls, and he desired me to tell him what to do. My reply was, '*Continue* to pray for your sons, and *expect* an answer to your prayer, and you will have to praise God.'

"Now, when after six years I was again in the same city, this dear man came to me and said he was surprised he had not seen before himself what he ought to do, and that he had resolved to take my advice and more earnestly than ever give himself to prayer.

"Two months after he saw me, five of his six sons were converted within eight days, and have for six years now walked in the ways of the Lord, and he had hope that the sixth son also was beginning to be concerned about his state before God.

"May the Christian reader be encouraged by this, should his prayers not at once be answered; and, instead of ceasing to pray, wait upon God all the more earnestly and perseveringly, and *expect* answers to his petitions."

THE DIVINE PLAN FOR SENDING OUT FOREIGN MISSIONARIES.

The Bristol Church with which Mr. Müller was connected has been privileged to set an example to the Church of God of the way in which Foreign Missionaries (who are so greatly needed) can be sent forth in answer to prayer. Mr. Müller writes on p. 516, Vol. I. of his Narrative:—

"I also mention here, that during the eight years previous to my going to Germany to labour there, it had been laid on my heart, and on the hearts of some other brethren among us, to ask the Lord that he would be pleased to honour us, as a body of believers, by calling forth from our midst brethren, for carrying the truth into foreign lands. But this prayer seemed to remain unanswered. Now, however, the time was come when the Lord was about to answer it, and I, on whose heart particularly this matter had been laid, was to be the first to carry forth the truth from among us. About that very time the Lord called our dear brother and sister Barrington from among us, to go to Demerara, to labour there in connexion with our esteemed brother Strong, and our dear brother and sister Espenett, to go to Switzerland. Both these dear brethren and sisters left very shortly after I had gone to Germany. But this was not all.

"Our much valued brother Mordal, who had commended himself to the saints by his unwearied faithful service among us for twelve years, had from Aug. 31, 1843, (the day on which brothers Strong and Barrington sailed from Bristol for Demerara), his mind likewise exercised about service there, and went out from among us eleven months after. He, together with myself, had had it particularly laid upon his heart, during the eight years previously, to ask the Lord again and again to call labourers from among us for foreign service. Of all persons he, the father of a large family, and about 50 years of age, seemed the least likely to be called to that work; but God did call him. He went, laboured a little while in Demerara, and then, on January 9, 1845, the Lord took him to his rest.—When we ask God for a thing, such as that He would be pleased to raise up labourers for His harvest, or send means for the carrying on of His work, the honest question to be put to our hearts should be this: Am *I* willing to go, if He should call *me*? Am *I* willing to give according to *my* ability? For we may be the very persons whom the Lord will call for the work, or whose means He may wish to employ."

In the Report of the Scriptural Knowledge Institution for 1896 Mr. Müller shows how greatly this body of believers has been honoured by God.

"From our own midst, as a church sixty brethren and sisters have gone forth to foreign fields of labour, some of whom have finished their labour on earth; but there are still about forty yet engaged in this precious service."

Why should not the great and crying need for workers in Asia, Africa, and other parts of the world be thus met by thousands of churches in Europe and America following this divine plan of praying the Lord of the harvest that He would send forth labourers from among them?

Surely they may expect GOD to answer their prayers as He did the prayers of this Bristol church.

Look what has been done in China by the faithful use of GOD'S method! We quote Mr. Hudson Taylor's words as given in *China's Millions* for July, 1897:—

"For the obtaining of fellow-workers we took the MASTER'S direction, 'Pray ye the LORD of the Harvest.' As for the first five before the Mission was formed, so for the twenty-four for whom we first asked for the C.I.M.; for further reinforcements when they were needed; for the seventy in three years, for the hundred in one year, and for further additions from time to time, we have ever relied on this plan. Is it possible that in any other way such a band of workers from nearly every denomination, and from many lands, could have been gathered and kept together for thirty years with no other bond save that which the call of GOD and the love of GOD has proved—a band now numbering over seven hundred men and women, aided by more than five hundred native workers."

THE BEGINNING OF THE 1859 REVIVAL.

"In November, 1856, a young Irishman, Mr. James McQuilkin, was brought to the knowledge of the Lord. Soon after his conversion he saw my Narrative advertised, viz.: the first two volumes of this book. He had a great desire to read it, and procured it accordingly, about January, 1857. God blessed it greatly to his soul, especially in showing to him, what could be obtained by prayer. He said to himself something like this: 'See what Mr. Müller obtains simply by prayer. Thus I may obtain blessing by prayer.'

"He now set himself to pray, that the Lord would give him a spiritual companion, one who knew the Lord. Soon after he became acquainted with a young man who was a believer. These two began a prayer-meeting in one of the Sunday Schools in the parish of Connor. Having his prayer answered in obtaining a spiritual companion, Mr. James McQuilkin asked the Lord to lead him to become acquainted with some more of His hidden ones. Soon after the Lord gave him two more young men, who were believers previously, as far as he could judge.

"In Autumn, 1857, Mr. James McQuilkin stated to these three young men, given him in answer to believing prayer, what blessing he had derived from my Narrative, how it had led him to see the power of believing prayer; and he proposed that they should meet for prayer to seek the Lord's blessing upon their various labours in the Sunday Schools, prayer-meetings, and preaching of the Gospel.

"Accordingly in Autumn, 1857, these four young men met together for prayer in a small school-house near the village of Kells, in the parish of Connor, every Friday evening. By this time the great and mighty working of the Spirit, in 1857, in the United States, had become known, and Mr. James McQuilkin said to himself, 'Why may not we have such a blessed work here, seeing that God did such great things for Mr. Müller, simply in answer to prayer.'

"On January 1, 1858, the Lord gave them the first remarkable answer to prayer in the conversion of a farm servant. He was taken into the number, and thus there were five who gave themselves to prayer. Shortly after, another young man, about 20 years old, was converted; there were now six. This greatly encouraged the other three who first had met with Mr. James McQuilkin. Others now were converted, who were also taken into the number; but only believers were admitted to these fellowship meetings, in which they read, prayed, and offered to each other a few thoughts from the Scriptures. These meetings and others for the preaching of the Gospel were held in the parish of Connor, Antrim, Ireland. Up to this time all was going on most quietly, though many souls were converted, There were no physical prostrations, as afterwards.

"About Christmas, 1858, a young man, from Ahoghill, who had come to live at Connor, and who had been converted through this little company of believers, went to see his friends at Ahoghill, and spoke to them about their own souls, and the work of God at Connor. His friends desired to see some of these converts. Accordingly Mr. James McQuilkin, with two of the first who met for prayer, went on February 2, 1859, and held a meeting at Ahoghill in one of the Presbyterian Churches.

"Some believed, some mocked, and others thought there was a great deal of presumption in these young converts; yet many wished to have another meeting. This was held by the same three young men on February 16th, 1859; and now the Spirit of God began to work, and to work mightily. Souls were converted, and from that time conversions multiplied rapidly. Some of these converts went to other places, and carried the spiritual fire, so to speak, with them. The blessed work of the spirit of God spread in *many places.*

"—On April 5th, 1859, Mr. James McQuilkin went to Ballymena, held a meeting there in one of the Presbyterian Churches; and on April 11th held another meeting in another of the Presbyterian churches. Several were convinced of sin and the work of the Spirit of God went forward in Ballymena.

"—On May 28th, 1859, he went to Belfast. During the first week there were meetings held in five different Presbyterian Churches, and from that time the blessed work commenced at Belfast. In all these visits he was accompanied and helped by Mr. Jeremiah Meneely, one of the three young men who first met with him, after the reading of my Narrative. From this time the work of the Holy Ghost spread further and further; for the young converts were used by the Lord to carry the truth from one place to another.

"Such was the *beginning* of that mighty work of the Holy Spirit, which has led to the conversion of hundreds of thousands; for some of my readers will remember how in 1859 this fire was kindled in England, Wales and Scotland; how it spread through Ireland, England, Wales and Scotland; how the Continent of Europe was more or less partaking of this mighty working of the Holy Spirit; how it led thousands to give themselves to the work of Evangelists; and how up to the year 1874 not only the effects of this work, first begun in Ireland, are felt, but that still more or less this blessed work is going on in Europe generally. It is almost needless to add, that in no degree the honour is due to the instruments, but to the Holy Spirit alone; yet these facts are stated, in order that it may be seen, what delight God has in answering abundantly the believing prayer of His children."

MR. MÜLLER'S MARRIAGE.

In Vol. 3 of The Narrative, Mr. Müller shows the ordering of God in his meeting with and subsequent marriage to his first wife, Miss Mary Groves.

"In giving her to me, I own the hand of God; nay, His hand was most marked; and my soul says, 'Thou art good, and doest good.' I refer to a few particulars for the instruction of others.

"When at the end of the year 1829, I left London to labour in Devonshire in the Gospel, a brother in the Lord gave to me a card, containing the address of a well-known Christian lady, Miss Paget, who then resided in Exeter, in order that I should call on her, as she was an excellent Christian. I took this address and put it into my pocket, but thought little of calling on her. Three weeks I carried this card in my pocket, without making an effort to see this lady; but at last I was led to do so. This was God's way of giving me my excellent wife. Miss Paget asked me to preach the last Tuesday in the month of January, 1830, at the room which she had fitted up at Poltimore, a village near Exeter, and where Mr. A. N. Groves, afterwards my brother-in-law, had preached once a month, before he went out as a Missionary to Bagdad. I accepted readily the invitation, as I longed, everywhere to set forth the precious truth of the Lord's return, and other deeply important truths, which not long before my own soul had been filled with.

"On leaving Miss Paget, she gave me the address of a Christian brother, Mr. Hake, who had an Infant Boarding School for young ladies and gentlemen, at Northernhay House, the former residence of Mr. A. N. Groves, in order that I might stay there on my arrival in Exeter from Teignmouth. To this place I went at the appointed time. Miss Groves, afterwards my beloved wife, was there; for Mrs. Hake had been a great invalid for a long time, and Miss Groves helped Mr. Hake in his great affliction, by superintending his household matters.

"My first visit led to my going again to preach at Poltimore, after the lapse of a month, and I stayed again at Mr. Hake's house; and this second visit led to my preaching once a week in a chapel at Exeter; and thus I went, week after week, from Teignmouth to

Exeter, each time staying in the house of Mr. Hake. All this time my purpose had been, not to marry at all, but to remain free for travelling about in the service of the Gospel; but after some months I saw, for many reasons, that it was better for me, as a young Pastor, under 25 years of age, to be married.

"The question now was, to whom shall I be united? Miss Groves was before my mind; but the prayerful conflict was long, before I came to a decision; for I could not bear the thought, that I should take away from Mr. Hake this valued helper, as Mrs. Hake continued still unable to take the responsibility of so large a household.

"But I prayed again and again. At last this decided me, I had reason to believe that I had begotten an affection in the heart of Miss Groves for me, and that therefore I ought to make a proposal of marriage to her, however unkindly I might appear to act to my dear friend and brother Mr. Hake, and to ask God to give him a suitable helper to succeed Miss Groves.

"On Aug. 15th, 1830, I therefore wrote to her, proposing to her to become my wife, and on Aug. 19th, when I went over as usual to Exeter for preaching, she accepted me. The first thing we did, after I was accepted, was, to fall on our knees, and to ask the blessing of the Lord on our intended union.

"In about two or three weeks the Lord, in answer to prayer, found an individual, who seemed suitable to act as housekeeper, whilst Mrs. Hake continued ill; and on Oct. 7, 1830, we were united in marriage. Our marriage was of the most simple character. We walked to church, had no wedding breakfast, but in the afternoon had a meeting of Christian friends in Mr. Hake's house and commemorated the Lord's death; and then I drove off in the stagecoach with my beloved bride to Teignmouth, and the next day we went to work for the Lord.

"Simple as our beginning was, and unlike the habits

of the world, for Christ's sake, so our Godly aim has been, to continue ever since. Now see the hand of God in giving me my dearest wife:—

"1st, that address of Miss Paget's was given to me under the ordering of God.

"2nd, I must at last be made to call on her, though I had long delayed it.

"3rd, She might have provided a resting-place with some other Christian friend, where I should not have seen Miss Groves.

"4th, My mind might have at last, after all, decided, not to make a proposal to her; but God settled the matter thus in speaking to me through my conscience —you know that you have begotten affection in the heart of this Christian sister, by the way you have acted towards her, and therefore, painful though it may be, to appear to act unkindly towards your friend and brother, you ought to make her a proposal. I obeyed. I wrote the letter in which I made the proposal, and nothing but one even stream of blessing has been the result.

"Let me here add a word of Christian counsel. To enter upon the marriage union is one of the most deeply important events of life. It cannot be too prayerfully treated. Our happiness, our usefulness, our living for God or for ourselves afterwards, are often most intimately connected with our choice. Therefore, in the most prayerful manner, this choice should be made. Neither beauty, nor age, nor money, nor mental powers, should be that which prompt the decision; but

"1st, Much waiting upon God for guidance should be used;

"2nd, A hearty purpose, to be willing to be guided by Him should be aimed after;

"3rd, True godliness without a shadow of doubt, should be the first and absolutely needful qualification, to a Christian, with regard to a companion for life.

"In addition to this, however, it ought to be, at the same time, calmly and patiently weighed, whether, in other respects, there is a suitableness. For instance, for an educated man to choose an entirely uneducated woman, is unwise; for however much on his part love might be willing to cover the defect, it will work very unhappily with regard to the children."

DANGEROUS ILLNESS OF MR. MÜLLER'S DAUGHTER.

"In July, 1853, it pleased the Lord to try my faith in a way in which before it had not been tried. My beloved daughter and only child, and a believer since the commencement of the year 1846, was taken ill on June 20th.

"This illness, at first a low fever, turned to typhus. On July 3rd there seemed no hope of her recovery. Now was the trial of faith. But faith triumphed. My beloved wife and I were enabled to give her up into the hands of the Lord. He sustained us both exceedingly. But I will only speak about myself. Though my only and beloved child was brought near the grave, yet was my soul in perfect peace, satisfied with the will of my Heavenly Father, being assured that He would only do that for her and her parents, which in the end would be the best. She continued very ill till about July 20th, when restoration began.

"On Aug. 18th she was so far restored that she could be removed to Clevedon for change of air, though exceedingly weak. It was then 59 days since she was first taken ill.

"Parents know what an only child, a beloved child is, and what to believing parents an only child, a believing child must be. Well, the Father in Heaven said, as it were, by this His dispensation, 'Art thou willing to give up this child to me?' My heart responded, As it seems good to Thee, my Heavenly Father. Thy will be done. But as our hearts were made willing to give back our beloved child to Him who had given her to us, so He was ready to leave her to us, and she lived. 'Delight thyself also in the Lord; and He shall give thee the desires of thine heart.' Psalm xxxvii.

"The desires of my heart were, to retain the beloved daughter if it were the will of God; the means to retain her were to be satisfied with the will of the Lord.

"Of all the trials of faith that as yet I have had to pass through, this was the greatest; and by God's abundant mercy, I own it to His praise, I was enabled to delight myself in the will of God; for I felt perfectly sure, that, if the Lord took this beloved daughter, it would be best for her parents, best for herself, and more for the glory of God than if she lived: this better part I was satisfied with; and thus my heart had peace, perfect peace, and I had not a moment's anxiety. Thus would it be under all circumstances, however painful, were the believer exercising faith."

THE DAILY BREAD.

"Aug. 3, 1844. Saturday. With the 12s. we began the day. My soul said: 'I will now look out for the way in which the Lord will deliver us this day again; for He will surely deliver. Many Saturdays, when we were in need, He helped us, and so He will do this day also.' Between nine and ten o'clock this morning I gave myself to prayer for means, with three of my fellow-labourers, in my house. WHILST WE WERE IN PRAYER, there was a knock at my room-door, and I was informed that a gentleman had come to see me. When we had finished prayer, it was found to be a brother from Tetbury, who had brought from Barnstaple £1 2s. 6d. for the Orphans. Thus we have £1 14s. 6d., with which I must return the letter-bag to the Orphan-Houses, looking to the Lord for more.

"Aug. 6.—Without *one single penny* in my hands the day began. The post brought nothing, nor had I yet received anything, when ten minutes after ten this morning the letter-bag was brought from the Orphan-Houses, for the supplies of to-day.—Now see the Lord's deliverance! In the bag I found a note from one of the labourers in the Orphan-Houses, enclosing two sovereigns, which she sent for the Orphans, stating that it was part of a present which she had just received unexpectedly, for herself.—Thus we are supplied for to-day.

"Sept. 4.—Only one farthing was in my hands this morning. Pause a moment, dear reader! Only one farthing in hand when the day commenced. Think of this, and think of nearly 140 persons to be provided for. You, poor brethren, who have six or eight children and small wages, think of this; and you, my brethren, who do not belong to the working classes, but have, as it is called, very limited means, think of this! May you not do, what we do, under your *trials*? Does the Lord love you less than He loves us? Does He not love all His children with no less love than that, with which He loves His only begotten Son, according to John xvii. 20-23? Or are we better than you? Nay, are we not in ourselves poor miserable sinners as you are; and have any of the children of God any claim upon God, on account of their own worthiness? Is not that, which alone can make us worthy to receive anything from our Heavenly Father, the righteousness of the Lord Jesus, which is imputed to those who believe in Him?

"Therefore, dear reader, as we pray in our every need, of whatever character it may be, in connection with this work, to our Father in Heaven for help, and as He does help us, so is He willing to help all His children who put their trust in Him.—Well, let us hear then, how God helped when there was only one farthing left in my hands, on the morning of Sept. 4, 1844.

"A little after nine o'clock I received a sovereign from a sister in the Lord, who does not wish the name of the place, where she resides, mentioned. Between ten and eleven o'clock the bag was sent from the Orphan-Houses, in which in a note it was stated that £1 2s. was required for to-day. SCARCELY HAD I READ THIS, when a fly stopped before my house, and a gentleman, Mr. ——, from the neighbourhood of Manchester, was announced. I found that he was a believer, who had come on business to Bristol. He had heard about the Orphan-Houses, and expressed his surprise, that without any regular system of collections, and without personal application to anyone, simply by faith and prayer, I obtained £2,000 and more yearly for the work of the Lord in my hands. This brother, whom I had never seen before; and whose name I did not even know before he came, gave me £2, as an exemplification of what I had stated to him."

"THE POOR WITH YOU ALWAYS."

"Feb. 12, 1845.—After I had sent off this morning the money which was required for the housekeeping of to-day, I had again only 16s. 2½d. left, being only about one-fourth as much as is generally needed for one day, merely for housekeeping, so that there was now again a fresh call for trusting in the Lord. In the morning I met again, as usual, with my dear wife and her sister, for prayer, to ask the Lord for many blessings in connection with this work, and for means also.

"About one hour after, I received a letter from Devonshire, containing an order for £22 of which £10 was for the Orphans, £2 for a poor brother in Bristol, and £10 for myself.—Besides having thus a fresh proof of the willingness of our Heavenly Father to answer our requests on behalf of the Orphans, there is this, moreover, to be noticed. For many months past, the necessities of the poor saints among us have been particularly laid upon my heart. The word of our Lord: 'Ye have the poor with you always,' and 'whensoever ye will ye may do them good,' has again and again stirred me up to prayer on their behalf, and thus it was again in particular this morning. It was the coldest morning we have had the whole winter. In my morning walk for prayer and meditation I thought how well I was supplied with coals, nourishing food, and warm clothing, and how many of the dear children of God might be in need; and I lifted up my heart to God to give me more means for myself, that I might be able, by actions, to show more abundant sympathy with the poor believers in their need; and it was but three hours after when I received this £10 for myself."

THE LORD DIRECTING THE STEPS.

"Feb. 1, 1847.—Before breakfast I took a direction in my usual morning's walk, in which I had not been for many weeks, feeling drawn in that direction, just as if God had an intention in leading me in that way. Returning home I met a Christian gentleman whom formerly I used to meet almost every morning, but whom I had not met for many weeks, because I had not been walking in that direction. He stopped me and gave me £2 for the Orphans. Then I knew why I had been led thus; for there is not yet enough in hand, to supply the matrons to-morrow evening with the necessary means for house-keeping during another week.

"Feb. 4.—Yesterday nothing had come in. This morning, just before I was going to give myself to prayer about the Orphans, a sister in the Lord sent a sovereign, which she had received, as she writes, 'From a friend who had met the Orphan Boys, and was particularly pleased with their neat and orderly appearance.' After having received this £1, I prayed for means for present use, though not confining my prayers to that. About a quarter of an hour after I had risen from my knees, I received a Setter, with an order for £5. The donor writes, that it is 'the proceeds of a strip of land, sold to the railway company.' What various means does the Lord employ to send us help, in answer to our prayers!"

CONTINUED TRIALS OF FAITH AND PATIENCE.

With the enlargement of the work, by which some 330 persons needed to be provided for, the trials of faith continued. Mr. Müller writes:—

"If we formerly had no certain income, so now have we none. We have to look to God for everything in connection with the work, of which often, however, the pecuniary necessities are the smallest matter; but to Him we are enabled to look, and *therefore* it is, that we are not disappointed."

"Oct. 7, 1852.—This evening there was only £8 left in hand for the current expenses for the Orphans. Hitherto we had generally abounded. But though much had come in, since the commencement of this new period, yet our expenses had been greater than our income, as every donation almost of which the disposal was left with me, had been put to the Building Fund. Thus the balance in hand on May 26, 1852, notwithstanding the large income since then, was reduced to about £8. I therefore gave myself particularly to prayer for means, that this small sum might be increased.

"Oct. 9.—This morning Luke vii came in the course of my reading before breakfast. While reading the account about the Centurion and the raising from death the widow's son at Nain, I lifted up my heart to the Lord Jesus thus: 'Lord Jesus, Thou hast the same power now. Thou canst provide me with means for Thy work in my hands. Be pleased to do so.' About half an hour afterwards I received £230 15s.

"The joy which such answers to prayer afford, cannot be described. I was determined to wait upon God only, and not to work an unscriptural deliverance for myself. I have thousands of pounds for the Building Fund; but I would not take of this sum because it was once set apart for that object. There is also a legacy of £100 for the Orphans two months overdue, in the prospect of the payment of which the heart might be naturally inclined to use some money of the Building Fund, to be replaced by the legacy money, when it comes in; but I would not thus step out of God's way of obtaining help. At the very time when this donation arrived, I had packed up £100 which I happened to have in hand; received for the Building Fund, in order to take it to the Bank, as I was determined not to touch it, but to wait upon God. My soul does magnify the Lord for His goodness.

"June 13, 1853.—We were now very poor. Not indeed in debt, nor was even all the money gone; for there was still about £12 in hand; but then there was needed to be bought flour, of which we buy generally 10 sacks at a time, 300 stones of oatmeal, 4 cwt. of soap, and there were many little repairs going on in the house, with a number of workmen, besides the regular current expenses of about £70 per week. Over and above all this, on Saturday, the day before yesterday, I found that the heating apparatus needed to be repaired, which would cost in all probability £25. It was therefore desirable, humanly speaking, to have £100 for these heavy extra expenses, besides means for the current expenses.

"But I had no human prospect whatever of getting even 100 pence, much less £100. In addition to this, to-day was Monday, when generally the income is little. But, in walking to the Orphan-House this morning, and praying as I went, I particularly told the Lord in prayer, that on this day, though Monday, He could send me much. And thus it was. I received this morning £301 for the Lord's service, as might be most needed.—The joy which I had cannot be described. I walked up and down in my room for a long time, tears of joy and gratitude to the Lord raining plentifully over my cheeks, praising and magnifying the Lord for His goodness, and surrendering myself afresh, with all my heart, to Him for His blessed service. I scarcely ever felt more the kindness of the Lord in helping me.

"Nov. 9.—Our need of means is now great, very great. The Lord tries our faith and patience. This afternoon, a brother and sister in the Lord, from Gloucestershire, called to see me at the New Orphan-House, before going through the house. After a few minutes I received from the sister a sovereign, which she had been requested to bring to me for the Building Fund; and she gave me from herself £1 for my own personal expenses, and £1 for the Building Fund, and her husband gave me £5 for the Orphans, and £5 for Foreign Missions.

"Thus the Lord has refreshed my spirit greatly; but I look for more, and need much more.

"Nov. 12.—This evening, while praying for means, came a little parcel, containing ten sovereigns, from a Christian lady, living not far from the New Orphan-House. This was a very great refreshment to my spirit.

"Oct. 17, 1854.—This morning at family prayer, came, in the course of reading, Exodus v, which shows that, just before the deliverance of the Israelites out of Egypt, their trials were greater than ever. They had not only to make the same number of bricks as before, but also to gather stubble, as no straw was given them any longer. This led me, in expounding the portion, to observe that even now the children of God are often in greater trial than ever, just before help and deliverance comes. Immediately after family prayer it was found, that by the morning's post not one penny had come in for the work of the Lord in which I am engaged, though we needed much, and though but very little had come in during the three previous days. Thus I had now to remember Exodus v, and to practice the truths contained therein. In the course of the day nothing was received. In the evening I had, as usual, a season for prayer with my dear wife, respecting the various objects of the Scriptural Knowledge Institution, and then we left the New Orphan-House for our home.

"When we arrived at our house, about nine o'clock, we found that £5 and also 5s. had been sent from Norwich in two Post Office Orders for the Building Fund, and that £8 3s. 11d. had been sent in for Bibles, Tracts, and Reports, which had been sold. This called for thanksgiving. But a little later, between nine and ten o'clock, a Christian gentleman called and gave me £1 for the Orphans and £200 for foreign missions. He had received these sums from an aged Christian woman, whose savings as a servant, during her WHOLE life, made up the £200, and who, having recently had left to her a little annual income of about £30, felt herself constrained, by the love of Christ, to send the savings of her whole life for foreign missions.

"Our especial prayer had been again and again, that the Lord would be pleased to send in means for missionary brethren, as I had reason to believe they were in much need of help; and only at eight o'clock this evening I had particularly besought the Lord to send help for this object. By the last mail I had sent off £40 to British Guiana, to help seven brethren there in some measure. This amount took the last pound in hand for this object. How gladly would I have sent assistance to other brethren also, but I had no more. Now I am in some degree supplied for this object.

"July 12, 1854.—Our means were now again reduced to about £30, as only about £150 had come in since June 15. In addition to this, we had very heavy expenses before us. This morning, in reading through the book of Proverbs, when I came to chapter xxii. 19 —'That thy trust may be in the Lord, &c.,' I said in prayer to Him: 'Lord, I do trust in Thee; but wilt Thou now be pleased to help me; for I am in need of means for the current expenses of all the various objects of the Institution.' By the first delivery of letters I received an order on a London bank for £100, to be used for all the various objects 'as the present need might require.'"

ARE YOU PREPARED FOR ETERNITY?

"In looking over my account books, I meet again and again with the name of one and another who has finished his course. Soon, dear reader, your turn and mine may come. Are you prepared for eternity? Affectionately I press this question upon you. Do not put it away. Nothing is of greater moment than this point; yea, all other things, however important in their place, are of exceedingly small importance, in comparison with this matter. Do you ask, how you may be prepared for eternity, how to be saved, how to obtain the forgiveness of your sins? The answer is, believe in the Lord Jesus, trust in Him, depend upon Him alone as it regards the salvation of your soul. He was punished by God, in order that we guilty sinners, if we believe in Him, might not be punished. He fulfilled the law of God, and was obedient even unto death, in order that we disobedient, guilty sinners, if we believe in Him, might, on His account, be reckoned righteous by God.

"Ponder these things, dear reader, should you have never done so before. Through faith in the Lord Jesus alone can we obtain forgiveness of our sins, and be at peace with God; but, believing in Jesus, we become, through this very faith, the children of God; have God as our Father, and may come to Him for all the temporal and spiritual blessings which we need. Thus everyone of my readers may obtain answers to prayers, not only to the same extent that we obtain them, but far more abundantly.

"It may be that few, comparatively, of the children of God are called to serve the Lord in the way of establishing Orphan-Houses, &c.; but all of them may, yea, are called upon to trust in God, to rely upon Him, in their various positions and circumstances, and apply the word of God, faith, and prayer to their family circumstances, their earthly occupation, their afflictions and necessities of every kind, both temporally and spiritually; just as we, by God's help, in some little measure seek to apply the word of God, faith and prayer to the various objects of the Scriptural Knowledge Institution for Home and Abroad. Make but trial of it, if you have never done so before, and you will see how happy a life it is.

"Truly I prefer by far this life of almost constant

trial, if I am only able to roll all my cares upon my Heavenly Father, and thus become increasingly acquainted with Him, to a life of outward peace and quietness, without these constant proofs of His faithfulness, His wisdom, His love, His power, His over-ruling providence, &c."

WAITING ONLY UPON GOD.

"Sept 6, 1854.—Received from Clerkenwell £50 to be used one-half for missions, and the other half as I thought best. I took the one-half for the support of the Orphans, and find the following remark in my journal respecting this donation: 'What a precious answer to prayer!' Since Aug. 26th we have been day by day coming to the Lord for our daily supplies. Precious, also, on account of Missionary brethren, whom I seek to help, for whom there was nothing in hand when this donation was received."

Mr. Müller adds a few remarks to this part of the Narrative:—

"1. Should anyone suppose, on account of its having been stated in the previous pages that we were repeatedly brought low as to means, that the Orphans have not had all that was needful for them; we reply that *never*, since the work has been in existence, has there a meal-time come, but the Orphans have had good nourishing food in sufficient quantity: and never have they needed clothes, but I have had the means to provide them with all they required.

"2. Never since the Orphan work has been in existence have I asked one single human being for any help for this work; and yet, unasked for, simply in answer to prayer, from so many parts of the world, as has been stated, the donations have come in, and that very frequently at a time of the greatest need."

Mr. Müller writes under date, 1859:—

"Every Wednesday evening I meet with my helpers for united prayer; and day by day I have stated seasons, when I seek to bring the work with its great variety of spiritual and temporal necessities, before the Lord in prayer, having perhaps each day 50 or more matters to bring before Him, and thus I obtain the blessing. I ask no human being for help concerning the work. Nay, if I could obtain £10,000 through each application for help; by God's grace, I would not ask. And why not? Because I have dedicated my whole life cheerfully to the precious service of giving to the world and to the church, a clear, distinct, and undeniable demonstration, that it is a blessed thing to trust in, and to wait upon, God; that He is now, as He ever was, the Living God, the same as revealed in the Holy Scriptures, and that if we know and are reconciled to Him through faith in the Lord Jesus, and ask Him in His name for that which is according to His mind, He will surely give it to us, in His own time, provided that we believe that He will.

"Nor has God failed me at any time. Forty years have I proved His faithfulness, in this work."

IN THE LORD JEHOVAH IS EVERLASTING STRENGTH.

Under date Nov. 9, 1861, Mr. Müller wrote:—

"Nov. 9. Saturday evening. When this week commenced, I received only £3 19s. by the first delivery. Shortly after there came in the course of my reading, through the Holy Scriptures, Isaiah xxvi, 4, 'Trust ye in the Lord for ever; for in the Lord Jehovah is everlasting strength.'—I laid aside my Bible, fell on my knees, and prayed thus: I believe that there is everlasting strength in the Lord Jehovah, and I do trust in Him; help me, O Lord, for ever to trust in Thee. Be pleased to give me more means this day, and much this week, though only so little now has come in.—That same day, Nov. 3rd, I received £10 from Surbiton, £5 from a donor residing in Clifton, £2 from a Bristol donor, and in the course of the week altogether £457 came in; thus Jehovah again proved, that in Him is everlasting strength, and that He is worthy to be trusted.—Dear believing reader, seek but in the same way to trust in the Lord, if you are not in the habit of doing so already, and you will find as I have found thousands of times, how blessed it is. But if the reader should be yet going on in carelessness about his soul, and therefore be without the knowledge of God and His dear Son, then the first, and most important thing, such a one has to do, is to trust in the Lord Jesus for the salvation of his soul, that he may be reconciled to God, and obtain the forgiveness of his sins."

JESUS CHRIST, THE SAME YESTERDAY, AND TODAY, AND FOREVER.

"May 26, 1861.—At the close of the period I find, that the total expenditure for all the various objects was £24,700 16s. 4d., or £67 13s. 5¾d. per day, all the year round. During the coming year I expect the expenses to be considerably greater. But God, who has helped me these many years, will, I believe, help me in future also.

"You see, esteemed reader, how the Lord, in His faithful love helped us year after year. With every year the expenses increased, because the operations of the Institutions were further enlarged; but He never failed us. You may say, however, 'What would you do, if He should fail in helping you?' My reply is, that cannot be, as long as we trust in Him and do not live in sin. But if we were to forsake Him, the fountain of living waters, and to hew out to ourselves broken cisterns, which cannot hold water, by trusting in an arm of flesh; or if we were to live in sin, we should then have to call upon Him in vain, even though we professed still to trust in Him, according to that word: 'If I regard iniquity in my heart, the Lord will not hear me.' Psalm lxvi, 18.

"Hitherto, by God's grace, I have been enabled to continue to trust in Him alone; and hitherto, though failing and weak in many ways, yet, by God's grace, I have been enabled to walk uprightly, hating sin and loving holiness, and longing after increased conformity to the Lord Jesus.

"Oct. 21 1868—As the days come, we make known our requests to Him, for our outgoings have now been for several years at the rate of more than One Hundred Pounds each day; but though the expenses have been so great, He has never failed us. We have indeed, as to the outward appearance, like the 'Burning Bush in the Wilderness;' yet we have not been consumed. Moreover, we are full of trust in the Lord, and therefore of good courage, though we have before us the prospect, that, year by year, our expenses will increase more and more. Did all my beloved fellow disciples, who seek to work for God know the blessedness of looking truly to God alone, and trusting in Him alone, they would soon see how soul refreshing this way is, and how entirely beyond disappointment, so far as He is concerned.

"Earthly friends may alter their minds regarding the work in which we are engaged; but if indeed we work for God, whoever may alter His mind regarding our service, He will not. Earthly friends may lose their ability to help us, however much they desire so to do; but He remains throughout eternity the infinitely Rich One. Earthly friends may have their minds after a time diverted to other objects, and, as they cannot help everywhere, much as they may desire it, they may, though reluctantly, have to discontinue to help us; but He is able, in all directions, though the requirements were multiplied a million times, to supply all that can possibly be needed, and does it with delight, where His work is carried on, and where He is confided in. Earthly friends may be removed by death, and thus we may lose their help, but He lives for ever, He cannot die. In this latter point of view, I have especially, during the past 40 years, in connection with this Institution, seen the blessedness of trusting in the Living God alone. Not one nor two, nor even five nor ten, but many more, who once helped me much with their means, have been removed by death; but have the operations of the Institution been stopped on that account? No. And how came this? Because I trusted in God, and in God alone."

THOROUGHLY IN HEART PREPARED FOR TRIALS OF FAITH.

Under date July 28, 1874, Mr. Müller wrote:—

"It has for months appeared to me, as if the Lord meant, by His dealings with us, to bring us back to that state of things, in which we were for more than ten years, from August, 1838, to April, 1849, when we had day by day, almost without interruption, to look to Him for our daily supplies, and, for a great part of the time, from meal to meal. The difficulties appeared to me indeed very great, as the Institution is now twenty times larger, than it was then, and our purchases are to be made in a wholesale way; but, at the same time, I am comforted by the knowledge, that God is aware of all this; and that, if this way be for the glory of His name, and for the good of His church and the unconverted world, I am, by His grace, willing to go this way, and to do it to the end of my course. The funds were thus fast expended; but God, our infinitely rich Treasurer, remains to us. It is this which gives me peace. Moreover, if it pleases Him, with a work requiring about £44,000 a year, to make me do again at the evening of my life, what I did from August, 1838, to April, 1849, I am not only prepared for it, but gladly again I would pass through all these trials of faith, with regard to means, if He only might be glorified, and His church and the world be benefited.

Often and often this last point has of late passed through my mind, and I have placed myself in the position of having no means at all left, and Two

Thousand and One Hundred persons not only daily at the table, but with everything else to be provided for, and all funds gone; 189 Missionaries to be assisted, and nothing whatever left; about one hundred schools, with about nine thousand scholars in them, to be entirely supported, and no means for them in hand; about Four Millions of Tracts and Tens of Thousands of copies of the Holy Scriptures yearly now to be sent out, and all the money expended. Invariably, however, with this probability before me, I have said to myself: 'God, who has raised up this work through me, God who has led me generally year after year to enlarge it, God who has supported this work now for more than forty years, will still help, and will not suffer me to be confounded, because I rely upon Him, I commit the whole work to Him, and He will provide me with what I need, in future also, though I know not, whence the means are to come.'

"Thus I wrote in my journal on July 28, 1874. The reader will now feel interested in learning how we fared under these circumstances.

"When I came home, last evening (July 27), I found letters had arrived, which contained £193, among which there was one from a Missionary in Foreign lands, helped by the funds of this Institution, who, having come into the possession of some money, by the death of a relative, sent £153 0s. 4d. for Foreign Missions. This morning, July 28, came in £24 more, so that, when I met this afternoon with several of my helpers for prayer for means and various other matters, such as spiritual blessing upon the various Objects of the Institution, for more rain in this very dry season, the health of our fellow-labourers, etc., we had received, since yesterday afternoon, altogether £217. We thanked God for it, and asked for more. When the meeting for prayer was over, there was handed to me a letter from Scotland, containing £73 17s. 10d., and a paper with 13s. This was the immediate answer to prayer for more means.

"Aug. 12.—The income for this whole week, since Aug. 5, has been £897 15s. 6½d.

"Sept. 16.—Just after having again prayed for the payment of legacies, which have been left, I had a legacy receipt sent for the payment of a legacy for £1,800.

"Sept. 23.—Income to-day £5,365 13s. 6d., of which there was sent in one donation £5,327 7s. 6d. The Lord be praised!"

STRONG IN FAITH, GIVING GLORY TO GOD.

On March 27, 1881, Mr. Müller found that no money remained in hand for the School, Bible, Missionary and Tract Funds. Nearly £1,400 had been spent for these Objects during the previous month. He writes:—

"What was now to be done, dear reader, under these circumstances, when all the money for the above Objects was again gone? I reply, we did what we have done for 47 years, that is, we waited continually upon God. My dear fellow-labourers in Bristol, and my dear wife and myself in America, brought our necessities again and again before the Lord.

"Here in the United States, besides our habitual daily prayer for help, we had especial seasons 4, 5, and 6 times a day additionally, for pouring out our hearts before our Heavenly Father, and making known our requests unto Him, being assured that help would come: and we have not waited upon the Lord in vain. This plan may be despised by some, ridiculed by others, and considered insufficient by a third class of persons; but, under every trial and difficulty, we find prayer and faith to be our universal remedy; and, after having experienced for half a century their efficacy, we purpose, by God's help, to *continue* waiting upon Him, in order to show to an ungodly world, and to a doubting Church, that the Living God is still able and willing to answer prayer, and that it is the joy of His heart to listen to the supplications of His children. In Psalm ix. 10, the Divine testimony regarding Jehovah is, 'They that know thy name will put their trust in Thee.' We know Him, by His grace, and do therefore put our trust in Him.

"April 27.—On March 27th we had no means at all in hand for these Objects, as stated under that date. We have now been helped through one more month, in answer to prayer, and have been supplied with all we needed, though that amounted to nearly £1000, and have £23 8s. 6¼d. left.

"April 29.—A servant of the Lord Jesus, who, constrained by the love of Christ, seeks to lay up treasure in heaven, having received a legacy of £532 14s. 5d., gave £500 of it for these Objects.

"July 28, 1881.—The income has been for some time past only about the third part of the expenses. Consequently, all we have for the support of the Orphans is nearly gone; and for the first four Objects of the Institution we have nothing at all in hand. The natural appearance now is, that the work cannot be carried on. But I BELIEVE that the Lord will help, both with means for the Orphans and also for the other Objects of the Institution, and that we shall not be confounded; also, that the work shall not need to be given up. I am fully expecting help, and have written this to the glory of God, that it may be recorded hereafter for the encouragement of His children. The result will be seen.

"The foregoing was written at 7 A. M. July 28, 1881. As yet we have the means to meet our expenses, and I expect that we shall not be confounded, though for seven years we have not been so poor."

The result has indeed been seen, and will be seen. For more than 20 years since those words were written and Mr. Müller had thus recorded his confidence in the Lord's help, God HAS sustained the work, and in May, 1902, there was a balance in hand of some thousands of pounds, notwithstanding that more than £500,000 had been received and expended since this entry was made in Mr. Müller's journal on July 28, 1881.

During these 20 years faith and patience were at times greatly tried:

"Aug. 15, 1881.—The balance for the Orphans is now reduced to £332 12s. 7d., lower than it has been for more than twenty-five years. This sum we have in hand to meet the daily expenses in connection with 2,100 persons. It is only enough for the average outgoings of 4½ days. But our eyes are upon the Lord. I look to my heavenly Provider. The total income of to-day has been £28 5s. 2½d.

"Aug. 22.—Part of a legacy, left years ago, £1,000, was paid, as the answer to many prayers.

"Feb. 26, 1882.—The balance in hand to-day for the Orphans is £97 10s. 7½d., viz., £24 more than the average expenses of one single day.

"March 2.—Our position now regarding the Orphan work is, praying day by day 'Give us *this day* our *daily* bread'. For a considerable time we have had day by day to look to the Lord for the supply of our *daily* wants; but God has helped us thus far.

"April 20, 1882.—When in the greatest need we received from Edinburgh £100 with this statement: 'The enclosed was intended as a legacy, but I have sent it in my lifetime.'

"June 3.—From Wottan-under-edge £500. A glorious deliverance was this donation, and a precious earnest of what God would do further for us.

"Oct. 21.—Received from Wottan-under-edge £1,000.

God, in answer to our prayers, spoke to His dear child, and inclined his heart to send to us more than ever. Thus He also gives proof, that during the previous year, when we were so low as to funds, it was only for the trial of our faith and patience, and not in anger; nor did He thereby mean to indicate, that He would not help us any more. For my own part, I *expected* further great help from God, and I have not been confounded.

"Aug. 17, 1883.—Our balance was reduced this afternoon to £10 2s. 7d. Think of this, dear reader! Day by day about 2,100 persons are to be provided for in the Orphan Institution, and £10 2s. 7d. was all that was in hand to do this. You see that we are just in the same position in which we were 46 years since as to funds. God is our banker. In Him we trust, and on Him we draw by faith. This was Saturday. In the evening £30 was received. On Monday we received £129 further, but had to pay out £60. On Tuesday we received £295, but had to pay out £180.

"God is pleased continually to vary His mode of dealing with us, in order that we may not be tempted to trust in donors, or in circumstances, but in Him alone, and to keep our eye fixed upon Him. This, by His grace, we are enabled to do, and our hearts are kept in peace."

Some ten months later, when the balance in hand was only £41 10s., a very little more than one-half of the average expenses for the Orphans for one day, and there were sanitary operations advisable to be carried out, the expenses of which would amount to upwards of £2,000, Mr. Müller received a legacy of £11,034 6s.

"June 7, 1884.—This is the largest donation I have *ever* received at *one time*. This legacy had been above six years in Chancery, and year after year its payment was expected, but remained unsettled by the Chancery Court. I kept on praying, however, and for six years prayed day by day that the money might be paid, believing that God in His own time (*which is always the best*), would help at last; for *many* legacies in Chancery I had prayed out of the Court, and the money was eventually paid. In the present case, too, after faith and patience had been sufficiently exercised, God granted this request likewise."

1893.—In the Fifty-fourth Report of the Scriptural Knowledge Institution Mr. Müller says:—

"The readers of the last report will remember, under what particular trials we entered upon the last financial year of the Institution, from May 26th, 1892, to May 26th, 1893; but we trusted in *God*; with unshaken confidence we looked to *Him*, and we *expected* that we should somehow or other be helped.

"While thus we went on, my heart was at peace habitually, being assured that all this was permitted by God, to prepare a blessing for thousands, who would afterwards read the record of His dealings with us, during the year from May 26th, 1892, to May 26th, 1893. With reference to our dear fellow-labourers, Mr. Wright and I have seen already, while passing through the trial, how God has blessed it to them.

"Aug. 30, 1892.—This evening, whilst reading in the Psalms, I came to Psalm lxxxi, 10, and remembered the work of the Holy Spirit in my heart, when reading this verse on Dec. 5, 1835, and the effect which this had, not only on leading me to found the greatest Orphan Institution in the world, but I thought also of the blessing which has thus been brought to tens of thousands of believers and unbelievers all over the world. Putting aside the Bible, therefore, I fell on my knees and asked God that He would graciously be pleased to repeat His former kindness, and to supply me again more abundantly with means. Accordingly in less than half an hour, I received £50 from a Bristol Donor and from Redland a large quantity of fish, in addition to £97 already received to-day as the result of much prayer. By the last delivery, at 9 p. m., I received £5 more also, and had thus £152 in all, this day, as the result of prayer.

"Nov. 11.—There came in to-day, by the first two deliveries, only about £8, but the Lord increased the income to more than £200 this day. I am never discouraged by very little only coming in, but say to myself, and also to my dear helpers, 'More prayer, more patience, and more exercise of faith will bring greater blessing'; for thus I have invariably found it, since October, 1830, now 63 years ago, when I first began this life of entire dependence upon God for everything.

"March 1, 1893.—The income during this week, ending to-day, was £92 8s. 8¾d. for the Orphans, and £9 11s. 2d. for the other Objects, being about the sixth part of our weekly expenses; but now the great trial of our faith was nearly brought to a close, as will presently be seen.

"March 4.—*This very day* God begins to answer our prayers, as we have received a very good offer for the land we have to sell, even £1,000 per acre. The beginning of the day was darker as to outward appearances than ever: but we trusted in God for help. The first three deliveries of letters brought us only £4, and the remaining three brought us so little that the whole day's income was only £8 instead of £90, the amount we require every day to meet all our expenses. But God has now helped us. We have been able this evening to sell ten acres of land and two-fifths of an acre at £1,000 per acre, and shall receive £10,405 altogether for the whole of one field. The contract was signed at 8 o'clock this evening."

MR. MÜLLER'S DEPARTURE TO BE WITH CHRIST.

On the evening of Wednesday, March 9th, 1898, Mr. Müller took part in the usual meeting for prayer held in the Orphan-House No. 3; retired at his usual hour to rest, and early on the following morning (the 10th of March) alone, in his bed-room, breathed his last, realising what had long been with him a most joyous anticipation, viz., that "to depart and to be with Christ is far better."

March 14.—This day Mr. Müller's earthly remains were laid in the grave of his first and second wives, at Arno' Vale Cemetery. The attendant circumstances, throughout, were very remarkable and interesting to the Christian mind chiefly as illustrating God's eternal principle—"Them that honour Me I will honour." The man who in life sought not his own glory, became in death the one to whom all classes delighted to show respect and honour.

From the masses of sympathising spectators that lined the streets, from the tearful eyes, and the audible prayerful ejaculations that escaped the lips of bystanders (many of them the poorest of the poor), as the orphans filed past, following the hearse; from the suspension of all traffic in the principal streets, the tolling of muffled bells, and the half-masted flags, and from the dense crowds in the cemetery that awaited the arrival of the funeral company, it seemed as if the whole city had spontaneously resolved to do honour to the man who had not lived for himself, but for the glory of God and the good of his fellows.

For some 21 months before Mr. Müller's death the trials of faith and patience were great. Mr. James Wright, Mr. Müller's successor, writes:

"He who is pleased, sometimes, to teach His servants 'how to *abound*,' sees it *best* for them, at other times 'to be instructed how to suffer need.' For many of the 64 years during which this work has been carried on, the former was our experience; we abounded and richly abounded, latterly, and especially during the last 2 or 3 years it has been the very reverse. *Pressing need* has been the *rule*; a balance in hand, over and above our need, the rare exception. Yet we have never been forsaken."

"Sept. 23, 1897.—Residue of the legacy of the late G. J., Esq., £2,679 18s. 7d. This sum was received when we were in the *deepest need*; and after it had pleased the Lord to allow a very protracted trial of faith and patience; but see, beloved reader, He did not disappoint nor forsake us, as He *never* does those who really trust in Him. The *joy* of *such* a deliverance cannot be tasted without the experience of the previous *trial*.

"Feb. 26, 1898.—The following entry, under this date, is in Mr. Müller's own hand-writing:

"The income to-day, by the two first deliveries, was £7 15s. 11d. Day by day our great trial of faith and patience continues, and thus it has been, more or less, now, for 21 months, yet, by Thy grace, we are sustained."

March 1, 1898.—The following, again, is from a memorandum in Mr. Müller's own hand-writing, under this date:

"For about 21 months with scarcely the least intermission the trial of our faith and patience has continued. Now, to-day, the Lord has refreshed our hearts. This afternoon came in, for the Lord's work, £1,427 1s. 7d. as part payment of a legacy of the late Mrs. E. C. S. For 3 years and 10 months this money had been in the Irish Chancery Court. Hundreds of petitions had been brought before the Lord regarding it, and now at last, this portion of the total legacy has been received."

Thus the Lord, in love and faithfulness, greatly refreshed the heart of His servant, only nine days before taking him home to be with Himself.

APPENDIX A
FIVE CONDITIONS OF PREVAILING PRAYER

1. Entire dependence upon the merits and mediation of the Lord Jesus Christ, as the only ground of any claim for blessing. (See John xiv. 13, 14; xv. 16, etc.)

2.—Separation from all known sin. If we regard iniquity in our hearts, the Lord will not hear us, for it would be sanctioning sin. (Psalm lxvi. 18.)

3.—Faith in God's word of promise as confirmed by His oath. Not to believe Him is to make Him both a liar and a perjurer. (Hebrews xi. 6; vi. 13-20.)

4.—Asking in accordance with His will. Our motives must be godly: we must not seek any gift of God to consume it upon our lusts. (1 John v. 14; James iv. 3.)

5.—Importunity in supplication. There must be waiting on God and waiting for God, as the husbandman has long patience to wait for the harvest. (James v. 7; Luke xviii. 1-8.)

APPENDIX B
THE CAREFUL AND CONSECUTIVE READING OF THE HOLY SCRIPTURES

CONCERNING this subject Mr. Müller says: "I fell into the snare, into which so many young believers fall, the reading of religious books in preference to the Scriptures. I could no longer read French and German novels, as I had formerly done, to feed my carnal mind; but still I did not put into the room of those books the best of all books. I read tracts, missionary papers, sermons, and biographies of godly persons.

"The last kind of books I found more profitable than others, and had they been well selected, or had I not read too much of such writings, or had any of them tended particularly to endear the Scriptures to me, they might have done me much good.—I never had been at any time in my life in the habit of reading the Holy Scriptures. When under fifteen years of age, I occasionally read a little of them at school; afterwards God's precious book was entirely laid aside, so that I never read one single chapter of it, as far as I remember, till it pleased God to begin a work of grace in my heart.

"Now the Scriptural way of reasoning would have been: God himself has condescended to become an author, and I am ignorant about that precious book, which His Holy Spirit has caused to be written through the instrumentality of His servants, and it contains that which I ought to know, and the knowledge of which will lead me to true happiness; therefore I ought to read again and again this most precious book, this book of books, most earnestly, most prayerfully, and with much meditation; and in this practice I ought to continue all the days of my life. For I was aware, though I read it but little, that I knew scarcely anything of it. But instead of acting thus, and being led by my ignorance of the word of God to study it more, my difficulty in understanding it, and the little enjoyment I had in it, made me careless of reading it (for much prayerful reading of the Word, gives not merely more knowledge, but increases the delight we have in reading it); and thus, like many believers, I practically preferred, for the first four years of my divine life, the works of uninspired men to the oracles of the living God. The consequence was, that I remained a babe, both in knowledge and grace. In knowledge I say; for all *true* knowledge must be derived, by the Spirit, from the Word.

"And as I neglected the Word, I was for nearly four years so ignorant, that I did not *clearly* know even the *fundamental* points of our holy faith. And this lack of knowledge most sadly kept me back from walking steadily in the ways of God. For it is the truth that makes us free, (John viii. 31, 32,) by delivering us from the slavery of the lusts of the flesh, the lusts of the eyes, and the pride of life. The Word proves it. The experience of the saints proves it; and also my own experience most decidedly proves it. For when it pleased the Lord in Aug. 1829, to bring me really to the Scriptures, my life and walk became very different. And though even since that I have very much fallen short of what I might and ought to be, yet, by the grace of God, I have been enabled to live much nearer to Him than before.

"If any believers read this, who practically prefer other books to the Holy Scriptures, and who enjoy the writings of men much more than the word of God, may they be warned by my loss. I shall consider this book to have been the means of doing much good, should it please the Lord, through its instrumentality, to lead some of His people no longer to neglect the Holy Scriptures, but to give them that preference, which they have hitherto bestowed on the writings of men. My dislike to increase the number of books would have been sufficient to deter me from writing these pages, had I not been convinced, that this is the only way in which the brethren at large may be benefited through my mistakes and errors, and been influenced by the hope, that in answer to my prayers, the reading of my experience may be the means of leading them to value the Scriptures more highly, and to make them the rule of all their actions.

"If anyone should ask me, how he may read the Scriptures most profitably, I would advise him, that:

"I.—Above all he should seek to have it settled in his own mind, that God alone, by His Spirit, can teach him, and that therefore, as God will be enquired of for blessings, it becomes him to seek God's blessing previous to reading, and also whilst reading.

"II.—He should have it, moreover, settled in his mind, that, although the Holy Spirit is the *best* and *sufficient* teacher, yet that this teacher does not always teach immediately when we desire it, and that, therefore, we may have to entreat Him again and again for the explanation of certain passages; but that He will surely teach us at last, if indeed we are seeking for light prayerfully, patiently, and with a view to the glory of God.

"III.—It is of immense importance for the understanding of the word of God, to read it in course, so that we may read every day a portion of the Old and a portion of the New Testament, going on where we previously left off. This is important—1, Because it throws light upon the connection; and a different course, according to which one *habitually* selects particular chapters, will make it utterly impossible ever to understand much of the Scriptures. 2, Whilst we are in the body, we need a change even in spiritual things; and this change the Lord has graciously provided in the great variety which is to be found in His word. 3, It tends to the glory of God; for the leaving out some chapters here and there, is practically saying, that certain portions are better than others: or, that there are certain parts of revealed truth unprofitable or unnecessary. 4, It may keep us, by the blessing of God, from erroneous views, as in reading thus regularly through the Scriptures we are led to see the meaning of the whole, and also kept from laying too much stress upon certain favourite views. 5, The Scriptures contain the whole revealed will of God, and therefore we ought to seek to read from time to time through the whole of that revealed will. There are many believers, I fear, in our day, who have not read even once through the whole of the Scriptures; and yet in a few months, by reading only a few chapters every day they might accomplish it.

"IV.—It is also of the greatest importance to meditate on what we read, so that perhaps a small portion of that which we have read, or, if we have time, the whole may be meditated upon in the course of the day. Or a small portion of a book, or an epistle, or a gospel, through which we go regularly for meditation, may be considered every day, without, however, suffering oneself to be brought into bondage by this plan.

"Learned *commentaries* I have found to store the *head*, with many notions and often also with the truth of God; but when the *Spirit* teaches, through the instrumentality of prayer and meditation, the *heart* is affected. The former kind of knowledge generally puffs up, and is often renounced, when another commentary gives a different opinion, and often also is found good for nothing, when it is to be carried out into practice. The latter kind of knowledge generally humbles, gives joy, leads as nearer to God, and is not easily reasoned away; and having been obtained from God, and thus having entered into the heart, and become our own, is also generally carried out."

APPENDIX C
PROVING THE ACCEPTABLE WILL OF GOD

IT IS VERY INSTRUCTIVE and helpful to see the way in which Mr. Müller proved the acceptable will of the Lord, when exercised in heart about the enlargement of the Orphan work, so that not only 300 but 1000 Orphans might be provided for.

"Dec. 11, 1850.—The especial burden of my prayer therefore is, that God would be pleased to teach me His will. My mind has also been especially pondering, how I could know His will satisfactorily concerning this particular. Sure I am, that I shall be taught. I therefore desire patiently to wait for the Lord's time, when He shall be pleased to shine on my path concerning this point.

"Dec. 26.—Fifteen days have elapsed since I wrote the preceding paragraph. Every day since then I have continued to pray about this matter, and that with a goodly measure of earnestness, by the help of God. There has passed scarcely an hour during these days, in which, whilst awake, this matter has not been more or less before me. But all without even a shadow of excitement. I converse with no one about it. Hitherto have I not even done so with my dear wife. From this I refrain still, and deal with God alone about the matter, in order that no outward influence, and no outward excitement may keep me from attaining unto a clear discovery of His will. I have the fullest and most peaceful assurance, that He will clearly show me His will. This evening I have had again an especial solemn season for prayer, to seek to know the will of God. But whilst I continue to entreat and beseech the Lord, that He would not allow me to be deluded in this business, I may say I have scarcely any doubt remaining on my mind as to what will be the issue, even that I should go forward in this matter.

"As this, however, is one of the most momentous steps that I have ever taken, I judge that I cannot go about this matter with too much caution, prayerfulness, and deliberation. I am in no hurry about it. I could wait for years, by God's grace, were this His will, before even taking one single step towards this thing, or even speaking to anyone about it; and, on the other hand, I would set to work to-morrow, were the Lord to bid me do so. This calmness of mind, this having no will of my own in the matter, this only wishing to please my Heavenly Father in it, this only seeking His and not my honour in it; this state of heart, I say, is the fullest assurance to me that my heart is not under a fleshly excitement, and that, if I am helped thus to go on, I shall know the will of God to the full. But, while I write thus, I cannot but add at the same time, that I do crave the honour and the glorious privilege to be more and more used by the Lord. I have served Satan much in my younger years, and I desire now with all my might to serve God, during the remaining days of my earthly pilgrimage. I am forty-five years and three months old. Every day decreases the number of days that I have to stay on earth. I therefore desire with all my might to work. There are vast multitudes of Orphans to be provided for.

"I desire that thus it may be more abundantly manifest that God is still the hearer and answerer of prayer, and that He is the living God now, as He ever was and ever will be, when He shall, simply in answer to prayer, have condescended to provide me with a house for 700 Orphans, and with means to support them. This last consideration is the most important point in my mind. The Lord's honour is the principal point with me in this whole matter; and just because that is the case, if He would be more glorified by my not going forward in this business, I should, by His grace, be perfectly content to give up all thoughts about another Orphan-House. Surely, in such a state of mind, obtained by the Holy Spirit, Thou, O my Heavenly Father, will not suffer Thy child to be mistaken, much less to be deluded! By the help of God I shall continue further, day by day, to wait upon Him in prayer concerning this thing, till He shall bid me act.

"Jan. 2, 1851.—A week ago I wrote the preceding paragraph. During this week I have still been helped, day by day, and more than once every day, to seek the guidance of the Lord about another Orphan-House. The burden of my prayer has still been, that He, in His great mercy, would keep me from making a mistake. During the last week the Book of Proverbs has come, in the course of my Scripture reading, and my heart has been refreshed, in reference to this subject, by the following passages: 'Trust in the Lord with all thine heart; and lean not unto thine own understanding. In all thy ways acknowledge Him, and He shall direct thy paths.' Prov. iii. 5, 6.

"By the grace of God I do acknowledge the Lord in my ways, and in this thing in particular; I have therefore the comfortable assurance that He will direct my paths concerning this part of my service, as to whether I shall be occupied in it or not. Further: 'The integrity of the upright shall preserve them; but the perverseness of fools shall destroy them.' Prov. xi. 3. By the grace of God I am upright in this business. My honest purpose is to get glory to God. Therefore I expect to be guided aright. Further: 'Commit thy works unto the Lord and thy thoughts shall be established.' Prov. xvi.

I do commit my works unto the Lord, and therefore expect that my thoughts will be established.—My heart is more and more coming to a calm, quiet, and settled assurance, that the Lord will condescend to use me yet further in the Orphan Work. Here, Lord, is Thy servant!"

Mr. Müller wrote down eight reasons against and

eight reasons for establishing another Orphan-House for Seven Hundred Orphans.

The following is his last reason for so doing:

"I am peaceful and happy, spiritually, in the prospect of enlarging the work as on former occasions when I had to do so. This weighs particularly with me as a reason for going forward. After all the calm, quiet, prayerful consideration of the subject for about eight weeks, I am peaceful and happy, spiritually, in the purpose of enlarging the field. This, after all the heart searching which I have had, and the daily prayer to be kept from delusion and mistake in this thing, and the betaking myself to the Word of God, would not be the case, I judge, had not the Lord purposed to condescend to use me more than ever in this service.

"I, therefore, on the ground of the objections answered, and these eight reasons FOR enlarging the work, come to the conclusion that it is the will of the blessed God, that His poor and most unworthy servant should yet more extensively serve Him in this work, which he is quite willing to do."

"May 24.—From the time that I began to write down the exercises of my mind on Dec. 5th, 1850, till this day, ninety-two more Orphans have been applied for, and seventy-eight were already waiting for admission before. But this number increases rapidly as the work becomes more and more known.

"On the ground of what has been recorded above, I purpose to go forward in this service, and to seek to build, to the praise and honour of the living God, another Orphan-House, large enough to accommodate seven hundred Orphans."

www.ingramcontent.com/pod-product-compliance
Lightning Source LLC
Chambersburg PA
CBHW052102070526
44584CB00017B/2302